NONPROFIT FUNDRAISING STRATEGIES

7 STRATEGIES TO CONSISTENTLY SECURE FUNDING
AND ENSURE YOUR ORGANIZATION DOESN'T FAIL –
USING GRANTS, GIFTS, DIGITAL, AND MORE . . .

JAMES RUELL

CONTENTS

Introduction   7

1. WHAT ACTUALLY IS FUNDRAISING
   AND WHY IS IT SO IMPORTANT?   15
   A Brief Overview of Fundraising   16
   Benefits of Fundraising   18
   Essential Fundraising Principles   21
   Popular Examples of Fundraising
   Innovatively   24
   Summary   27

2. THE ESSENTIAL TOOLS OF A
   FUNDRAISER   29
   Benefits of Fundraising Tools   30
   The Tools of a Successful Fundraiser   32
   CRMs for Donor Management   36
   Peer-to-Peer Fundraising Platforms   38
   Summary   44

3. THE PLANNING STAGE   47
   Set Your Targets   49
   Select a Strategy   49
   Build a Plan   52
   Create a Budget   54
   Assemble a Team   55
   Execute   56
   Follow Up   57
   Summary   57

4. STRATEGY #1: THE PARTNERSHIP   59
   The Benefits of Partnerships and
   Collaborations for Nonprofits   60
   Exploring Different Types of Partnerships   64

How Can Your Partner Support Your
Nonprofit?   66
What Can Your Nonprofit Offer?   68
10 Steps to Securing Quality Partnerships   69
Summary   76

5. STRATEGY #2: BRINGING IN DONORS   79
Why Are Donors So Important?   81
The Importance of Loyal Donors   82
The 6 Main Types of Donors   84
How to Bring in Donors for a Fundraiser   88
Summary   93

6. STRATEGY #3: THE DIGITAL
FUNDRAISER   95
The Role of Social Media in Fundraising   96
Digital Platforms for Fundraising   99
Social Media Advertising   102
Digital Fundraising   104
10 Steps for a Successful Digital Fundraiser   107
Summary   111

7. STRATEGY #4: THE CAMPAIGN   113
What Are Campaigns and Why Are They
So Important?   114
Types of Fundraising Campaigns   116
9 Steps to Organize Successful Fundraising
Campaigns   119
Summary   123

8. STRATEGY #5: ANNUAL GIVING   125
Why Is Annual Giving So Important for
Nonprofits?   126
Types of Annual Fund Programs   128
12 Steps to Successfully Fundraise with
Annual Incentives   130
Summary   136

9. STRATEGY #6: EVENT HOSTING   139
   Types of Fundraising Events   141
   13 Steps to Hosting a Successful Event   145
   Summary   151

10. STRATEGY #7: DONOR RETENTION
    AND MANAGEMENT   153
    What Is Donor Retention and Why Does It
    Matter?   154
    Donor Stewardship   156
    11 Steps to Maintaining Donor Retention   159
    Summary   165

11. 11. THE FUNDRAISING FAQ   167
    How do you ask for donations?   168
    Are there certain rules on how much
    fundraising a nonprofit can do?   169
    How does a nonprofit get registered to
    fundraise?   169
    What do we need to know about raising
    funds beyond state lines?   170
    What can we do to ensure the success of
    our fundraising campaign?   171
    How do we ensure that our campaigning is
    completely legal?   172
    What information must we include in our
    fundraising materials?   173

    Conclusion   175
    Notes   179
    Other Books by James Ruell   181
    References   183

HOW TO GET A FREE COPY OF THE ULTIMATE 4-WEEK FUNDRAISE WORKBOOK

Would you like a copy of *The Ultimate 4-Week Fundraise Workbook*?

Get free and unlimited access to the below ebook and all of my future books by joining my community.

Scan with your camera to join.

INTRODUCTION

> "*Fundraising is the gentle art of teaching the joy of giving.*"
>
> — HANK ROSSO

You're exhausted, frustrated, and stressed. After years of leading a nonprofit, your go-to fundraising tactics just aren't bringing in as much as they used to—and nowhere near what your operating costs call for. The main question that weighs on your mind, and your small team, grows increasingly urgent with each passing day: How do we bring in more donations to stay afloat? You're a tight-knit group who toil tirelessly in service of the mission. When the essence of your goals and intentions is this pure—to help your local community—should just staying open one more day really be what you're worrying about? Unfortunately, it is.

Nonetheless, you're constantly overworked and over-whelmed by fundraising. The regular calendar of events requires a grueling amount of late-night and weekend work to organize, manage, and plan. And even before the onset of the pandemic—which sent demand for your services skyrocketing – income from the usual campaigns had already been on a slow but steady decline. The fundraisers you've relied on for years just aren't bringing in as much money as they used to. Surely there's a better way . . .

Sound familiar? I've experienced this, and there is a better way. The cycle of fundraising stress and being overwhelmed, while common—no wonder so many wind up leaving the sector altogether—doesn't need to be a certainty. There are easier, better ways to fundraise—and you don't need to scour the web to piece together random techniques to experiment with. Instead, from years of research and practice, I've pulled them all together in one book that you can reference time and time again. You'll learn the foundational best practices that I've learned from personal experience and that every fundraiser needs to know, as well as practical action steps that will start bringing money in the door.

How do I know what works? How can I help you with this? While we may never cross paths in real life, I know very well the hardship you face when it comes to fundraising. If we have never met before, it's a pleasure to meet you. I feel honored that you have picked up my book and I will do my best to pay you back for your trust. If every person who reads this book is able to raise just a little bit more money for their nonprofit then I will consider it a success. But I won't stop there; I am confident that if you read this book and apply the methods within, you will raise much more than 'just a little bit,' and on a much more consistent basis. Regardless, many of the tips, tricks, and ideas within will be applicable to your nonprofit with minimal effort and amazing results. But don't trust me, you'll need to see for yourself.

My name is James and I've served as a Director of an award-winning charity for several years. When I first joined the charity we were a small, modest charity whose impact was limited to the local government housing estate that our office resided within. Fast-forward a few years and we have more than doubled our income and, more importantly, our impact on our local community. This didn't come without struggle and a lot of learning, but with the recognition of a lot of large governmental and philanthropic organizations, the sleepless nights are fewer and further between.

With my experience in this charity's finances over the past few years, I can say with absolute confidence that it's entirely possible to build a sustainable, thriving nonprofit with the right fundraising strategies.

My background lies in finance. Although finance and nonprofits have traditionally been on opposite ends of the business spectrum, what I've learned is that nonprofits tend to suffer from a lack of research and investment that for-profit businesses would normally benefit from. The allure of large profits means that for-profit businesses suck up all the financial resources and investment, leaving nonprofit organizations perpetually underserved. Now, I'm dedicated to bridging this gap to help the charity sector expand and support nonprofit leaders in managing their organizations efficiently. My previous book, *Winning Grants: How to Write Winning Grant Proposals That Will Get You Funding for Your Nonprofit,* serves as a definitive manual for grant writing across sectors—and is a great companion to the one you're reading right now.

This is your shortcut to a sustainable fundraising blueprint. I'll break down 7 core fundraising strategies, diving deep into the most effective way to organize, plan, and execute each method. Each strategy is fully fleshed out, with detailed, practical action steps and insights to help you raise funds the right way for your nonprofit.

Success is not that far away, no matter what it might feel like right now. Follow the formulas outlined in the chapters ahead and the results will speak for themselves.

You'll quickly become well versed in fundraising techniques and be able to see which ones map best to your organization as I did for mine. Your team will learn invaluable lessons from the first rollout and, subsequently, develop the capability to deploy the strategies again and again so that you can create income streams you can count on. You'll be able to deploy the strategies any time your nonprofit needs a cash infusion, knowing that they will deliver a return—rather than hoping and wishing. Rinse and repeat. These reliable sources of funding will become the lifeblood of your nonprofit, allowing you to grow and reach even more of those who most need your services. Imagine expanding your mission to match your highest goals instead of turning them away, downscaling projects to match available resources, or parking ideas indefinitely.

Like me, you care deeply about those you serve. You know that despite all the good work your nonprofit does, it's just a drop in the ocean compared to what's possible. And you know the key lies in unlocking more funding and creating more reliable income streams.

In picking up this book, you've already shown that you're with me and you're serious about doing this. It's easy to bemoan the limitations we have to work with; not as easy to shift gears and embrace new ways of thinking and operating. To get different results, we must do something different, and step out of our comfort zones.

The deeper in you get, the more value you'll uncover as we dive into each of the 7 strategies and what it takes to succeed with each. Any and all of these strategies will work. It's up to you to choose which ones will be most effective for your nonprofit and go all in on applying them.

You're going to learn the building blocks of effective campaigning and how to utilize them to your benefit. I'll explain exactly what goes into preparing for a fundraiser, and walk you through the execution phase, step-by-step. I'll also introduce you to the world of part-nerships. This is an often overlooked channel, but there are so many opportunities in this space once you know what to look for in a mutually beneficial partnership. Collaboration is central to success in the nonprofit field, and that applies at the individual level as well as at the macro level.

Of course, donors are essential to any nonprofit, so we'll devote some time to understanding the role they play, and how you can make it impossible for them to say no. Naturally, one key way to connect with donors today is through social media. We'll go through the various online platforms available, their strengths and features, and how you can leverage the world of digital to your advantage.

Campaigns remain an important source of funding. Certain factors may not be immediately obvious when it comes to effectively collecting funds through campaigning. We'll cover how to use campaigns to their full potential, bringing in both likely partners and donors. Likewise, annual giving can form an important part of the overall funding puzzle. I'll help you tap into this market effectively and your organization can start generating steady income on a regular basis.

Events have always been a mainstay of the fundraising scene. They're highly engaging, although often labor-intensive. You'll find out how to maximize return on your events while minimizing effort through strategic planning and execution.

And although it's easy to overlook donor retention, maintaining a healthy relationship with major donors and partners is vital to reduce the amount of ongoing work you need to do to fundraise for your nonprofit. We'll cover some best practices in this area while making them as simple and easy as possible to shore up your retention and, ultimately, financial resilience.

Once you pick a path, keep the momentum going. Take action—do something. Most people stop at consuming.

It's one thing to absorb information, but what makes a difference is what you do with your new knowledge. Going one step further and implementing these methods are what will set you apart and ensure the success of your nonprofit.

We'll begin with a quick overview of the state of fundraising today. What exactly is fundraising and why does it matter? And once we establish the many benefits of fundraising, we'll explore some inspiring examples of innovative fundraising to get your own creative juices flowing.

If, like me, you are an active learner, then I highly recommend you download this book on Audible and listen to it in tandem. Your retention of the information contained within and your ability to recall it when you need it will be much higher and ultimately lead to you becoming a more successful fundraiser.

Let's get on with it and officially begin the next phase in your fundraising journey.

1

WHAT ACTUALLY IS FUNDRAISING
AND WHY IS IT SO IMPORTANT?

C an you guess how many nonprofits never make it past the 10-year mark . . . 1%, 5%, or 15%? Data from the National Center on Charitable Statistics (Ebarb, 2019) suggests that around 30% of nonprofits fail after 10 years. Many flounder due to a lack of strategic planning. It's not uncommon for nonprofit leaders to have blind spots when it comes to external forces and factors that ultimately become their downfall. After all, when you're laser-focused on the immediate needs of those you serve, and the daily crises that tend to erupt out of nowhere and require your full attention to solve, there isn't much bandwidth left over to stay attuned to the broader picture. Often, we don't think of other nonprofits as being our competitors, even though, ultimately, they're also vying for the same attention and dollars. We may fall prey to mission creep; after all, there are so many needs out there and so many deserving recipients. Or we might struggle to adapt our programs to meet evolving needs and keep up with the changing landscape. Sometimes we simply miscalculate what it truly takes to execute our mission. Although 'business plan' isn't part of the nonprofit lexicon, the same principles apply to our sector. It probably won't surprise you to hear that fundraising strategy and sustainability are rated as the top challenges among nonprofits, according to the Ewing Marion Kauffman Foundation (2017).

Where sales are the lifeblood of a typical company, fundraising is the lifeblood of a nonprofit. Longevity requires a sustainable funding strategy. In this chapter, we'll explore the nature of fundraising, the fundamental principles at play, and how fundraising has helped countless people across the world. You'll come away with a fresh appreciation for the art of fundraising, and a few ideas from other innovative charitable fundraising techniques to set you up for what comes next.

A BRIEF OVERVIEW OF FUNDRAISING

Let's start with a quick definition of fundraising. Simply put, it's the process of collecting money from donors, which could be either individuals or organizations— foundations, corporations, and even governments. And why do nonprofits need to fundraise? It's in the name. Nonprofits don't generate a surplus to benefit shareholders. Any profit is funneled back into the organization. Without fundraising, they wouldn't be able to function. After all, those served by nonprofits are not in a position to pay for the essential services received. Keep in mind that the main purpose of any nonprofit is to provide a public benefit of some type. Yet, nonprofits need funds to cover everything from wages and salaries to operating expenses for their premises and programs. Ultimately, the more money they raise, the more good they can do in their given field, whether that's supporting underprivileged populations, environmental causes, human or animal rights, disaster relief, rare diseases, or whatever their focus might be. So if there's one thing nonprofits have in common, it's that fundraising must be a top priority to ensure their long-term survival. While they can qualify for tax exemptions and may receive benefits like discounts on the goods and services required to run their operations, there is no getting around the fact that it takes cash to keep things running.

Those in the profession of raising funds are known as fundraisers. However, fundraising within a nonprofit also includes responsibilities such as managing relationships with donors, managing volunteers, managing event logistics, and more. Their remit is broad. Likewise, fundraising is about much more than simply soliciting donations from others. There's much more to it. Nonprofits benefit in a variety of ways that go beyond the financial aspect.

For starters, fundraising helps to build awareness of your nonprofit. As you expand your reach—connecting with more people—and as that emotional bond grows, you'll find they are more likely to support your mission. Not just that, they may give more frequently, in larger amounts, or engage on a deeper level, perhaps even volunteering time and other resources as well. Donor loyalty is a wonderful byproduct of increased interest in your nonprofit more generally.

You can see how fundraisers provide a wonderful way to reach out to potential supporters, grow your donor base, recruit volunteers, and raise your nonprofit's profile. Not only that; the advantages flow both ways.

BENEFITS OF FUNDRAISING

As we just established, increasing awareness of your charity and your cause is a major reason to fundraise. That increased brand recognition can also lead to more media coverage and opportunities, further extending your visibility. After all, in order for people to give, they first need to know about your nonprofit. If they aren't aware of your existence, there's no way for them to pledge support. Fundraising helps get your name in front of more fresh eyes, as well as reminding existing supporters about how they can continue to help. Taking a step back, fundraising serves to lift awareness around your purpose as well. The people, animals, or causes you serve can all benefit from more of the public knowing about their needs, too.

Speaking of the public, fundraising is one way you can recognize the contributions and efforts of supporters and say thank you. Their commitment to supporting a cause makes your nonprofit's work possible. Charitable donations can be tax-deductible. But the bigger payback for donors is mental and emotional. Studies show that giving makes us feel better (Suttie & Marsh, 2010). The feel-good factor that comes with helping others is based in science. Doing good in the world stimulates the release of chemicals like dopamine, serotonin, and oxytocin into our brains. Giving back and the subsequent sense of making a tangible difference is actually beneficial for donors. It's one of the most fulfilling things we can do as humans. For corporations, participating in charitable fundraisers is also a great way to generate goodwill for their brand. It can engender positive feelings internally with staff, as well as externally with customers and other stakeholders.

Fundraisers create a space to bring together different communities in the name of positive change. Fundraising events offer an opportunity for the public to meet with your staff and volunteers, get a better insight into what you do, and see firsthand what direct impact their contribution could have. They bring your staff and stakeholders together, creating a sense of shared momentum and community, and raising morale. Fundraising provides a chance to make useful connections and collaborate with other like-minded organizations. It also offers an opportunity to ensure alignment on priorities and values. Likewise, this gives individuals donating their time or money a chance to meet other like minds who share similar interests and beliefs. Many friendships have grown from simply connecting through an event like a walk-a-thon. In fact, fundraisers can be a great introduction to something you have always wanted to try—swimming? baking?—but never quite got around to.

Conversely, fundraising can be an overlooked avenue for professional development. Every event is a team-building exercise in its own right, requiring everyone to pitch in and often pick up some new skills along the way. Volunteering time can provide an opportunity to share knowledge and practice skills in everything from administration and project management to marketing, copywriting, social media, and event management. There is even the possibility of making new professional connections that could lead to more doors opening in the future. Any time you create an opportunity for people to come together, you create the conditions for exciting possibilities like these.

So, when we give people the chance to make a difference simply by giving money or time, there's in actual fact a two-way value exchange at play. Giving back makes us feel productive as well as more connected to those around us. These social ties feed into both improved mental and physical health. It's also worth noting here that when someone gives, they also spur a ripple effect throughout their community, inspiring others to act in similar ways (Suttie & Marsh, 2010). This ultimately creates a compounding of altruism—what you might call the butterfly or domino effect.

ESSENTIAL FUNDRAISING PRINCIPLES

Now that we've established the purpose and importance of fundraising for nonprofits, let's examine a few essential principles you need to know to successfully raise funds.

Always begin by developing a motive and statement. What do you hope to achieve? Why—how will this tie into your mission? How do you intend to achieve this result? How is your charity placed in terms of capacity and capability to carry out the plan? What type of budget do you have to work with, and who will pay for the costs? Start with the outcome in mind and methodically work your way through the next steps, one at a time.

Focus on building impactful relationships. Keep your audience at the forefront. Consider their motivations and how you can best meet their needs. Where do they spend their time? How do they like to engage? How much do they know about your charity? What would be meaningful to them? People give in order to see the impact of their contribution, not just because they see a cause that needs support. The more effort you put into understanding them upfront, the more likely you are to be rewarded as a result. Cultivate connections before asking for anything. Lead by informing and educating. Always be respectful of their decisions to give or not, and their preferences around privacy and receiving communications.

Maintain a high degree of transparency and accountability. It takes time to gain trust but very little time to lose it. And once eroded, that credibility is difficult to regain. Protect your public reputation by acting with integrity, following any legal or regulatory requirements, and prioritizing the interests of supporters where appropriate. Be honest, truthful, and upfront whenever you are representing your nonprofit, particularly regarding how funds are spent. Be clear and precise about your work, how donations are managed, and how costs and impact shake out. Where donors indicate how they would like their contributions used, follow those wishes, and engage with them about alternatives if this is not possible. Disclose any conflicts of interest and decline gifts that would not be in the interests of your organization, supporters, or beneficiaries.

Act responsibly. Balance and manage your responsibilities, understanding the wider charitable landscape we operate within. Hold yourselves and others to high ethical and operating standards, including suppliers and partners. For example, ensure fundraisers are fairly remunerated, declare any gratuities they are offered, and do not receive disproportionate personal gain. This is how we raise the bar on fundraising excellence while demonstrating respect for donors and maintaining accountability—building their confidence in us so we can continue to ask for their support in the future.

These are just a few high-level concepts to keep in mind as you get deeper into this book. You'll get a full playbook later on with much more detail on every single step of the fundraising process, from soup to nuts. In the meantime, let's take a quick detour into some inspirational examples of innovative fundraising.

POPULAR EXAMPLES OF FUNDRAISING INNOVATIVELY

There is no shortage of tried-and-true fundraising tactics out there to follow—membership drives, mail appeals, telethons, events, and the list goes on. These are popular, established methods for a reason. But every so often, new, novel campaigns launch that capture public interest and make a real splash.

Remember the Ice Bucket Challenge? Videos popped up all over the internet of people pouring buckets full of icy water over their heads. Why? It was all in the name of raising awareness and funds for amyotrophic lateral sclerosis, more commonly abbreviated as ALS—also known as Lou Gehrig's disease (named after the baseball player). The general notion was that participants nominated someone else to take part, and if they failed to do so, they could forfeit by making a charitable donation. The tagging or calling out of friends to douse themselves in turn, made the campaign feel highly personal. It also helped fuel the spread of the campaign. The nature of the campaign also made for some rather entertaining videos.

ALS activists Patrick Quinn and Pete Frates co-founded the challenge, which went viral over the summer of 2014 (Frates went on to write a book about the Ice Bucket Challenge and his own experience with ALS). According to the *New York Times*, more than 1.2 million videos were shared on Facebook over a six-week period, and the campaign was mentioned more than 2.2 million times on Twitter with hashtags such as #IceBucketChallenge, #ALSIceBucketChallenge, and #StrikeOutALS (Steel, 2014). Wikipedia pages on ALS also saw massive increases in traffic during this time. All in all, the ALS Ice Bucket Challenge raised $115 million in donations. Since 2014, the ALS Association has committed more than $131 million toward its mission, including over $118 million for worldwide research collaborations (ALS, 2021).

The pandemic called for many nonprofits to get creative with their usual fundraisers. The charity DigDeep had everything lined up and ready to go ahead of its fundraiser for World Water Day in 2020—on March 22, to be precise. Nobody could have predicted a global pandemic throwing a spanner in the works. But they were determined to see things through in service of their $90,000 fundraising goal to ensure all Americans have access to clean running water.

DipDeep and their agency partner CauseMic devised a way to refocus the campaign strategy. The communication centered around an urgent, timely message, tying into the importance of handwashing and hygiene during COVID-19. With sanitation in the spotlight like never before, it was a prime time to raise awareness that not everyone has access to clean water. The campaign strategy also doubled down on leveraging DigDeep's database. The multi-channel approach spanned email, social media, text messaging, donation platform Funraise, and direct mail, enabling personalized messaging through segmentation and optimization. The strategy paid off, ultimately bringing in close to $150,000 in donations—blowing well past the original goal.

Or take the CFTK dance marathon. In North Carolina, the UNC Children's Hospital is served by the Carolina For The Kids Foundation, providing financial, medical, and emotional support to patients and their families. CFTK's annual dance marathon has been going for over 20 years and has become an institution of its own. But just as in the previous example, COVID-19 forced the foundation to rethink things. Historically, the event has consisted of an epic no-sleeping, no-sitting 24-hour event on the campus of UNC-Chapel Hill. But given worries about physical proximity to others and the fact that the campus had to shut down, CFTK adopted a digital approach, turning the dance marathon into a virtual format instead. This also helped save on production costs.

Let's look at one last example. Wings for Life, a charity supporting research into spinal cord injuries, put a unique spin on the classic charity run. Rather than compelling participants to achieve a certain distance, they simply had to see how far they could get within 30 minutes. After the half-hour was up, a chaser car set off, and once it caught up to them, then their race was deemed complete. The Wings for Life World Run 2021 raised more than 4 million euros for its cause and attracted a lot of attention thanks to its unusual rules.

In today's digital age where content can spread around the world almost instantly, the power of a popular viral campaign can't be underestimated. People crave novelty, and nonprofits that successfully harness the element of surprise and delight can go far with their fundraising efforts.

SUMMARY

Nonprofits, rather than selling goods or services as a business, would provide public benefits and rely on donations to do so. These contributions can come from individuals or organizations, who in turn benefit from the strong sense of satisfaction and fulfillment that comes with giving back.

Fundraising is central to the success of any nonprofit. Not only does it help your organization meet its funding needs so you can deliver your services and programs, but fundraising also serves other equally important needs, like creating buzz and awareness and cultivating community goodwill—all of which in turn feed into a flywheel for sustainable success.

Next, let's turn to the tools you'll need to kick off an effective fundraising program.

2

THE ESSENTIAL TOOLS OF A FUNDRAISER

> *"Alone we can do so little; together we can do so much."*
>
> — HELEN KELLER

Fundraising is a team sport. It's not an activity you undertake alone. You'll also need the right tools for the job. Just like a mechanic, doctor, chef, or builder relies on their go-to gear, you should develop your own set of tools and maintain them well. This chapter is devoted to exploring the tools of the trade, so you can start automating more tasks and processes, reach new audiences, and ultimately solicit more donations for your nonprofit.

BENEFITS OF FUNDRAISING TOOLS

Let's start with an obvious one. You can raise money through all sorts of platforms. Donations serve as the fuel for your mission, so the wider you can cast your net, the better. For example, online crowdfunding platforms like GoFundMe have a large user base already that you can tap into, who are already primed for charitable giving. We'll dive into specific platforms in a bit more detail later in this chapter. Greater visibility is another benefit. Marketing and promotion may not come naturally, but it's essential for any organization, especially those that ultimately rely on the goodwill of others. If people aren't aware of your nonprofit, or your name isn't top of mind for them, they're unlikely to give.

You can also nurture better connections with donors, which is essential for cultivating loyalty. These days, connections are frequently made and maintained online. People are more digitally active than ever. Here are two telling statistics. According to Pew Research, 85% of Americans go online on a daily basis—and 31% say they are "almost constantly" online (Perrin & Atske, 2021). Make sure you're meeting your donors where they are. That doesn't mean your nonprofit needs to be constantly posting content. You don't have to be on every social media platform. Simply be strategic about where, when, and how you show up in order to stay relevant to your audience, and when they engage, continue to engage with them to keep the conversation going.

Detailed reports on gifts, funds, and campaigns are one of the top benefits that fundraising tools can offer. All good tools will incorporate in-depth analysis capability to help you analyze your results and refine your approach. You should expect to be able to tweak or create your own custom reports based on your needs, serving up more detailed insights that help you spot trends, and make better decisions to optimize future campaigns.

Finally, the right tools can enable faster communication and more cost-effective planning. We've highlighted the role technology can play in communicating more closely with donors and prospects. It can also help when it comes to communicating with staff and stakeholders. Internal communication can become fragmented, especially as your nonprofit grows, so don't overlook this area when considering what tools you might want to leverage. And of course, planning and managing projects and campaigns can always benefit from having a solid, central point where all key action steps and resources are housed. General communication and project management tools will typically get the job done here; the same principles apply to both private and public sector needs.

THE TOOLS OF A SUCCESSFUL FUNDRAISER

Many nonprofits cobble together various general business software programs to run their operations but quickly run into limitations when it comes to the fundraising side of things. Keeping track of donations and mailing lists can get unwieldy fast. That's where specialist software comes in. Fundraising software comes in many guises and there are plenty of tools out there targeted at nonprofits. Some are complex and include a wide array of features, while others are more single-minded, specializing in one or just a few aspects of fundraising.

Investing in fundraising software will pay off. In a survey, 99 percent of nonprofit professionals said that having fundraising software in place positively impacted the total amount of donations they collected (Finch, 2015). Once you determine your needs, assess the available solutions, and decide on which options will help you accomplish your goals, you'll be able to start simplifying and streamlining your current processes. This doesn't just go for online fundraising. It can apply to in-person outreach and events as well. This will reduce the amount of work you need to put into your campaigns, double handling or busywork relating to backend processing and create more free time to focus on high-value tasks.

How, exactly, you might ask? Here are some of the main ways.

Software can make it easy to set up attractive campaign pages that showcase the need for donations. Donation forms usually provide a way to instantly give via credit card or other payment options. Usually, these collect donor contact details and allow them to select an amount and choose a one-off or recurring gift. Donation buttons serve as a call to action that link to your donation page and can be placed in strategic positions on various pages. If you're running some kind of event, then fundraising tools can help with building a landing page, enabling registrations, selling tickets if it's a paid event, communicating with attendees, and generating reports about the event.

Every donation should be swiftly acknowledged with a thank you of some kind. Everyone likes to have their generosity acknowledged, and these days, they expect it —quickly. Ideally, if someone donates on your website, they would receive a receipt by email almost instantly. It may take some time and effort to set up the right technology for this workflow initially, but once it's done, it will create a much better donor experience. You want to nurture a relationship with the aim of converting a one-off donor into a regular donor. This is an area to invest in.

Collecting donations is one key area. Another is managing donor information, and we'll explore CRM systems in more detail shortly. Fundraising tools can play a key role in helping you reach the right people at the right time with the right message. The more you automate the managing and tracking of your communications and campaigns, the more ROI you'll see. Without the right tools in place, your ability to scale will be limited. Put simply, you can reach more people and make a targeted ask with the help of software that helps you build and maintain lists of prospects. You should be able to narrow them down by frequency or recency of giving, zero in on anyone who gave last year but not this year, and so forth. You can then personalize your communications based on what you know about who you're targeting. Remember the Pareto principle; 80% of your donations typically come from 20% of your donor base. Filter your database, cultivate your best prospects, and focus your efforts.

Fundraising software can also help with processing donations. A gift could be automatically acknowledged with a receipt and then sent to your accounting software, saving you from doing these steps manually, and eliminating the risk of human error. Look for a program that can handle various types of donations, such as pledges, credits, in-kind donations, split gifts, restricted gifts, or matched gifts. Most general-purpose accounting software isn't built to handle these types of gifts. Consider how donors like to give, and how you can enable that. Let's say someone wants to sign up for a regular monthly pledge. In that case, you'll need a solution that can handle the recurring charge, ensuring it's processed each month, that the funds are then transferred to your account, and triggering a donor receipt.

Given that most people own and use mobile phones on a daily basis, consider setting up a text-to-give channel. Collecting donations via text message creates another simple avenue for fundraising, both for campaigns and ongoing efforts. Another digital tool to consider harnessing is crowdfunding. This is when you rally a large number of people to contribute to your cause, usually online. Crowdfunding can supplement your existing initiatives, or you might set up standalone crowdfunding campaigns. We'll cover the power of peer giving toward the end of this chapter.

Note that payment processor Stripe has special charity pricing for registered nonprofits, as well as advanced reporting tools. PayPal includes nonprofits in its Giving Fund, offering another way for people to discover your cause, and it integrates with many CRM solutions. Square's own CRM can sort donors by giving criteria, so you can contact segments based on their engagement with your organization.

Specialized software can help you analyze your tactics, breaking down campaigns and channels, yielding actionable insights to inform your next efforts. There are even prospect research tools that offer wealth screening— taking data from the public domain, analyzing trends, and pinpointing potential donors who could be good targets.

For nonprofits that rely on grants or are interested in building up this source of funding, there is dedicated grant management software to help you stay on top of applications. You can set up and assign tasks, reminders, and deadlines. If it's difficult keeping tabs on proposals and funding status—it's easy for these to fall through the cracks when you have many other things on your plate— let technology assist you so that you can submit more funding requests and increase your odds of success.

CRMS FOR DONOR MANAGEMENT

Customer relationship management (CRM) software can provide a single centralized hub with a unified view of all contacts—not just donors, but volunteers, beneficiaries, and other stakeholders. It can serve as a one-stop shop for follow-up tasks, too. Most are cloud-based, so anyone in your organization can access the information anytime, anywhere. Some CRMs do involve a bit of a learning curve, so factor this into your planning.

One of the top benefits a CRM offers is an easily accessible home for complete donor information. A CRM system can track basic information, like someone's name and contact details, as well as a full track record of their historic involvement with your nonprofit. Beyond just giving history, you should be able to see their relationships with each other. Your database, for example, might include various members of the same family, or multiple employees of the same company. If you knew Michael and Betty both work for Acme Corp, and that Michael's employer matches his donations, then it's safe to assume that the same would apply to Betty. This is a much more dynamic and user-friendly option compared to spreadsheets. Building sophisticated user profiles and tracking their interactions with your organization calls for a more robust tool. This way, you can build stronger relationships and communicate more effectively and efficiently.

Use your CRM to segment contacts and deploy targeted communications. Take into account communication preferences, giving preferences, event engagement, business affiliations, and other relevant factors when individualizing newsletters, appeals, and receipts.

Importantly, a CRM should be able to produce a range of high-level reports, as well as provide granular insights into individual profiles. These will help you better understand your supporter base and refine your fundraising plans. How often do donors give? How much do they give at a time? These are questions a CRM can help answer. And you'll be able to track the results of campaigns—which you can also share with donors to demonstrate the impact of their contributions.

PEER-TO-PEER FUNDRAISING PLATFORMS

Peer-to-peer (P2P) fundraising is a specific type of crowdfunding and a relatively new arrival on the scene. Today, anyone can set up a fundraising page online and solicit donations for a cause. That means individuals can create their own fundraisers on behalf of your nonprofit, tailoring their appeals based on their personal experiences. They then share these online, through email and social media, spreading the word and collecting donations. The funds raised may go toward a specific campaign, or to your overall organization. You'll often see these in action when someone is doing a charity race, for example, or even taking part in a campaign like Movember, when people grow mustaches in the month of November in support of men's health issues, such as prostate cancer or testicular cancer.

P2P can be a highly effective strategy for raising funds. One key advantage is the opportunity to acquire new donors. P2P fundraising creates an organic extension of your organizational fundraising efforts. Individuals share their fundraising page with their family members, friends, and other peers, which could ultimately net your nonprofit fresh donors who are new to the cause. Their networks start to become your networks, too. These types of fundraisers ultimately hinge on personal connections—the trust between the person raising funds and their peers who choose to donate. After all, aren't you more likely to give to a cause when you know someone close to you supports it?

It would be unrealistic to expect every single contact of yours to donate to your P2P fundraiser. That said, getting people to talk about a cause is a huge step in the right direction. Raising awareness, fostering dialogue, and encouraging sharing are all great wins. Make sure individuals have the information they need to talk accurately and powerfully about your mission, so they can help educate their networks. Many of those contacts are likely to want to learn more about your nonprofit (and may even go on to contribute after that). Optimize all your social media profiles to capitalize on the increased attention. Encourage people to like and follow, or sign up to your email list, so you can continue to communicate with them and stay in their orbit. Growing your social media presence is a worthy secondary goal for any P2P campaign.

To really capitalize on the increased brand exposure, ensure that key elements of individual P2P campaign pages retain your nonprofit's branding. Visual attributes will do most of the heavy lifting in terms of brand recognition, so pay attention to your logo, typeface, colors, and images. Keep these elements consistent across campaign pages, fundraising pages, donation checkout pages, and all other touch points. Between a strong brand identity and a known, trusted giving platform, people will be more likely to feel comfortable pulling out their credit cards.

When a P2P campaign ties in with an event, it can also help bump up attendance numbers as well as raise funds. If you use dedicated event software, see if it connects to your P2P fundraising platform, so you can share data and streamline workflows. For example, you could then invite your P2P donors to your event. The P2P funds could help pay for the event itself or be added to the total amount raised through the event.

Think of P2P supporters as ambassadors for your organization. Treat this as an opportunity to learn more about them. They will often include personal notes on their fundraising pages about why your cause means so much to them, which is a valuable insight into their motivations that you can record in your donor database. It's this level of personal connection that makes P2P fundraising so successful. They're willing to share their beliefs and values widely, putting a personal face (their own) to your cause. So, be sure to reach out and thank them for their efforts after their campaign ends. They've bought into your mission deeply enough to go out and solicit on your behalf, and that deserves acknowledgment.

P2P can be a low-cost way for your organization to expand its reach and build credibility with more potential supporters. Campaigns are run entirely online, requiring little from your staff, so they can continue working on other initiatives during this time.

It offers a way for individuals to support a nonprofit without necessarily giving their own money, instead leveraging the trust they have with their networks. The proof is in the numbers. For instance, the average fundraiser on the DonorPerfect platform raises $568 (Orlando, 2021). And there are many other platforms you can use:

- **Qgiv** is a comprehensive fundraising platform catering to online and P2P fundraising as well as events, including auctions and mobile bidding. Set up branded event pages, email campaigns, leaderboards, live fundraising thermometers, milestone badges, and more. It can integrate with your CRM, email marketing platform, QuickBooks, and other programs—to name a few.

- **Salsa** provides a host of features for fundraising, advocacy, donor and event management, and marketing automation. It closely integrates with Salesforce. P2P features include individual and team donation pages, event registration pages, coaching messaging, content syndication to related organizations, and widgets to enable corporate employee donation matching.

- **Springly** is an all-in-one nonprofit management software focused on membership experience. That includes CRM, event management, fundraising and membership capability, and communication tools.

- **Fundly** is designed for online campaigns, with fundraising pages heavily featuring photo and video galleries and slideshows—you can add content straight from Facebook, YouTube, and Vimeo. Donation forms can be integrated directly into Facebook.

- **Grassroots Unwired** caters to mobile canvassing and constituent engagement, as well as fundraising, event management, and donations. Its 4EventDay app packs in a host of features like participant check-in, real-time connection with your CRM, offline capability, and simple sales and donations.

- **OneCause** offers a range of features and reporting for events, from planning and promotion through to ticketing, tables, registration, and checkout. Online fundraising is covered, too, with their virtual fundraising features, as well as text-to-give, silent auctions, and mobile bidding.

- **Donately**'s fundraising solution, as the name might suggest, prioritizes the donor experience. Along with fundraising pages, you can build multistep forms, embed them on popular website platforms like WordPress and Squarespace, and accept payments through a range of providers including Apple Pay and PayPal. Donately also integrates with tools like HubSpot and Google Analytics.

- **Classy** allows for flexible fundraising pages with photo, video, and blog updates, along with inbuilt social sharing, live leaderboards, and progress charts. The platform provides encouraging tips and coaching for fundraisers, and you can set up your own tailored versions through email for them.

- **GoFundMe** is perhaps the best-known and most popular P2P platform, often used to raise funds for personal emergencies as well as charitable organizations. It is free to use, with a transaction fee automatically deducted from each donation. GoFundMe offers access to a global community of more than 100 million people. Charities can also access donor and fundraiser reports.

- **Bonfire**'s unique fundraising platform lets supporters create and share T-shirt fundraisers on your behalf, using the Bonfire graphic library and product catalog, with all the money going to your nonprofit. You can highlight individual campaigns on your organizational profile, be notified about every new campaign, and see details about each supporter.

- **Funds2Orgs** is another niche platform for shoe drive fundraisers—collecting new or lightly worn shoes. These are then picked up and sent overseas to developing countries, primarily to women-owned micro-enterprises. Funds2Orgs provides a welcome kit and weekly tips, plug-and-play social media posts, templates, and a dedicated fundraising coaching team.

SUMMARY

While fundraising is ultimately about connecting with other people, technology can do a lot of the heavy lifting for you. Make sure you stay up to date with the latest tools available and how they can help your nonprofit save time and money. You'll be able to fundraise much more efficiently when you leverage these to their full capacity. There are many excellent general fundraising software programs on the market, as well as specialist CRMs to assist with donor management, and an ever-growing list of peer-to-peer fundraising platforms to take advantage of.

When scoping out potential tools to integrate into your operations, consider the size of your organization and the skill set of your existing staff. Smaller nonprofits may not need all the bells and whistles of a more comprehensive program, for example. Look for free trials so you can test run tools, checking how user-friendly they are and how well their features mesh with your needs. Some may only support online activity, for instance, while others cater to a wider range of use cases. Take the time upfront to determine what are must-haves for your nonprofit, which are nice-to-haves, and don't get dazzled by flashy features that don't tick these boxes. Consider your existing tools and whether they can integrate to create a more seamless experience for you and your staff.

Now, you're ready to move on to the next phase: planning. It's time to shift gears and drill into how successful fundraisers are actually executed.

3

THE PLANNING STAGE

As the saying goes—failing to plan is essentially planning to fail. You need to know what you're aiming for if you want to get somewhere. Once you digest this chapter, you will be equipped to avoid this surprisingly common downfall. Particularly when you're working with limited resources, it's essential to make the most of them. The good news is, working within constraints can often breed creative solutions.

Good strategic planning will help your organization achieve its goals. These should flow out of your nonprofit's overall mission—your driving force. If your mission is to support new immigrants in education, a goal might be to offer scholarships for them, and an objective could be to award 10 scholarships over the next year. See how that provides a clear direction? Then, you can evaluate your assets and pinpoint any challenges. A SWOT analysis, for example, will highlight strengths, weaknesses, opportunities, and threats. Armed with all this information, you'll be well placed to create a strategic plan and a work plan to use moving forward.

When it comes to fundraising, planning well ahead will be the key to success. Consider this. When you're planning a fundraiser, what you're essentially doing is setting up and operating a small business venture. A temporary one, with a short shelf life—in fact, you know the exact date that it will be wound up—but an unarguably commercial one, nonetheless. Given that you only have a short time to drum up support, putting in the time upfront to plan things out could be the make-or-break factor. Organizing things as you go, especially when dealing with a large-scale project, is a recipe for stress. The more you can plan beforehand, in as much detail as possible, the more your future self will thank you. Get a head start, especially on the most time-consuming tasks, and make things easier for your whole team down the track.

So, what is the best way to approach planning your next fundraiser?

SET YOUR TARGETS

Start by defining your priorities. No doubt your nonprofit has a multitude of needs but narrow it down to one specific need that you'll raise funds for. Maybe, as in the early example, it's to fund scholarships for new immigrants.

Define a concrete financial goal for your fundraiser. How will you measure success? Look to achieve a balance between setting your sights high versus choosing a comfortable number that you know you can easily surpass. You might set a reasonable topline target which seems within the reach of possibility, as well as a stretch goal that reflects bigger hopes. Think ambitious yet achievable. Consider what other goals you may hope to tick off through this fundraiser as well, such as increasing donor acquisition and donor retention. There may also be other areas you would like to tackle, such as growing community engagement or building closer ties with staff and volunteers, which don't necessarily map to clear metrics.

SELECT A STRATEGY

Once you establish the amount you want to raise, it's time to think about how you'll achieve this. Where might this money come from? Brainstorm likely sources. How much might come from businesses, and which ones? What about grants? Who can you lean on within and beyond your community? What tactics will you employ to hit your funding goal this year? What about next year or the year after that? Can you roll out the same blueprint again, tweaking based on learnings from each iteration?

Choose what type of fundraiser to execute. (Over the next few chapters, we'll break down 7 specific strategies in detail.) Consider the mission of your organization, the talent and skills at your disposal, and your key audiences. These should all align; the intersection of these three elements will help determine what type of fundraiser you should select for the best chance of success. This decision could be made with broad consultation, or at the management level. Either way, give the matter the time it deserves.

Have you run a similar fundraiser before? Have your competitors? How was the public response? Will staff or volunteers require training? Do you have the tools and technology you need to pull this off? Will you need to solicit volunteers? Will you have enough funds to cover the costs? Are your best donors more likely to attend a gala or auction, a family-friendly fair, or a walk-a-thon? Are they time-poor and more inclined to simply write a check or donate online? Asking questions like these will help you zero in on the right type of fundraising strategy.

Whether you are focusing on individual giving, group giving, or corporate giving, among the most common techniques are online campaigns, direct mail, and tele-marketing. Many nonprofits hold one or two special events a year, which presents an opportunity to mobilize supporters who otherwise wouldn't engage, whether in person, virtually, or through a hybrid approach. Events can run the gamut from small to large and can include participatory events (such as walks, races, or cook-offs). And of course, grant funding is another avenue you can pursue, although the timelines and outcomes here will be beyond your control. Avoid relying heavily on only one type of fundraising, especially if that source could suddenly dry up, putting your nonprofit's financial health in jeopardy. But conversely, spreading your efforts too thin—going too wide with a scattergun approach—is unlikely to result in success.

Identify the key message for your fundraiser, which again will be informed by your mission and goal. Don't get bogged down by the details. Instead, focus on the why—ending discrimination or hunger, protecting animals, providing employment, etc. Highlight the donor's role in all this; their contributions enable the work—they are the real heroes. Reinforcing this consistently will help make it clear why people should support your cause, inspire them to act, and help them to spread the word, too. A rousing message is ultimately what will spur people to give.

Note for US nonprofits: You may need to register in any relevant states before going any further. Most states today require nonprofits to do so before asking for donations from their residents.

BUILD A PLAN

Now, it's time to translate the strategy into a concrete plan—a campaign calendar. A solid plan gives you a reference to work from, serving as the sole source of truth for everyone involved in making this fundraiser happen. When you're in the midst of juggling all the logistics, this will be a sanity saver. The combination of documented tasks and timelines will help when motivation starts to flag, or the team starts to lose focus.

Set a start and end date for your project, factoring in sufficient preparation time as well as some time afterward for reflection and analysis. In the preliminary stages of planning, you might specify milestones like "mid-October," and adjust these to specific dates closer to the time as the plan takes shape. Your plan should include labor time, as this will require a significant commitment from your staff and potentially volunteers. Be as thorough as you can. Note down anything that needs to be accounted for, no matter how minor. It's a clever idea to schedule any labor-intensive events or initiatives early in the campaign when energy levels tend to be at their highest.

When planning how to promote your fundraiser and get traction, choose your channels strategically. How can you reach those who are most likely to give, purchase, register, attend, and spread the word? There are traditional media like TV, radio, and print, as well as posters and flyers, and of course direct mail and phone. Online, there are plenty of options, from email and social media to paid digital advertising and partnering with influencers. Plan to start promoting a few weeks before your fundraiser officially begins, to build interest and get word of mouth flowing.

Then you can dig into brainstorming any hurdles that may get in the way and slow you down. Do you anticipate running into certain challenges based on previous experience? Is gaining media attention often a struggle? What about connecting with specific target audiences, like Generation Z? Or donor retention? Once you establish the main concerns, how could you go about proactively addressing these?

CREATE A BUDGET

You know what type of fundraiser you want to deliver, and how much you want to raise through it. Now, it's time to consider how much it will cost your organization to execute. The larger the initiative, the more resources it is likely to consume. But even the leanest campaigns still require an investment of time and money. Getting these projections right will be critical if you hope to hit your fundraising goal. Any blowouts will impact your profit.

If you've previously planned and delivered similar fundraisers, retrieve data from those. Look at the budget and the performance of the iterations that came before to anchor your next one—revenue, expenses, profit, and how these compared to the original goal.

Once you have come up with estimates for all expenses, work out the projected net revenue. Refer back to the goal—your original target for this fundraiser. If there is a gap between these numbers, then it's time to get to work to make up the shortfall. This could mean cutting back on certain costs or aiming to raise more. Calculate how your team could balance project spending to maximize the end profit.

As you refine your budget and work plan, bringing the details into sharper focus, adjust your plans accordingly. It's especially important to account for any additional costs that arise. Adding branded merchandise to the strategy? Incorporate line items for designing, manufacturing, and shipping.

For major campaigns, break down your revenue goals by phase. For example, the majority of funds may be raised through major gifts early on.

ASSEMBLE A TEAM

Bring together a project team who will execute the fundraiser together. They don't need to be experts in fundraising, but they should bring to the table skills that will help propel the campaign forward. For example, some key skills that will prove valuable include marketing, communications, writing, public relations, social media, design, photography, and videography. An external expert can be a useful addition to the project team as well. For example, you might bring in a consultant to assist with planning, researching key donors, or helping with turning the plan into concrete actions. Be transparent about why everyone is there, so they can make the best contribution. As you recruit more people, you can use their commitment to rally others to join the team, too. Highlight the impact you plan to make with your fundraiser and the anticipated benefits. Be clear about what you're asking of them. Set expectations upfront and respect their time and energy.

Effective delegation will be essential to success. Break down the various workstreams and assign specific to-dos to your staff. Defining clear roles and responsibilities for each team member will empower them to take decisive action and keep things moving forward. Certain areas can be designated the domain of an individual or a small group–depending on their interests and strengths. Create key performance indicators (KPIs) for people where it makes sense. For example, a team member might aim to pitch to a certain number of prospects by a certain date. These KPIs can be mapped out and aligned with the overall project timeline.

EXECUTE

Once everyone is clear on what they need to do, and when, the wheels are really in motion—procuring the materials and locations for events, creating collateral, setting up donation pages and forms, and so forth. Project leaders should check in regularly with team members. Of course, conducting group meetings is a must, but individual check-ins are important, too. This can help with identifying any issues early on, taking preventive or corrective action, and ensuring things progress according to the timeline.

Once launch day rolls around, you'll start to see all your hard work pay off. This stage is usually incredibly gratifying after the weeks or months of toiling behind the scenes. So, be sure to track and celebrate progress during this phase. Individuals can keep a running tally of how many prospects they've contacted or how much money they've raised to date.

FOLLOW UP

Your plan should also account for closing things off post-fundraiser. After your campaign wraps up, it's not over just yet. This is the point when you review the total amount raised and share the results. Hold a debrief session to go over what went well, and what could have been improved, but keep the focus positive and congratulatory. Reward the team for all their hard work. Think about how best to show your appreciation, depending on how individuals prefer to be recognized. In some cases, coming together to celebrate as a group may be appropriate. And of course, thank anyone else who contributed to the fundraiser's success, like partners, suppliers, board members, and major donors.

SUMMARY

Pulling off a successful fundraiser takes work and a lot of planning. If you want to reach and exceed your goals, you'll need to set clear objectives, be realistic about the resources at hand, and devise a detailed plan, complete with granular tasks and deadlines that ladder up to the official public launch of your campaign. And of course, you will need to assemble a team of enthusiastic experts to help deliver it. After the fundraiser ends, be sure to document any lessons learned, so you can refine and improve when it's time to do it all again.

Next, we will start to investigate specific strategies for raising funds. I've selected the best, most efficient strategies to highlight over the coming chapters. As we touched on briefly, there are many tried-and-tested methods to solicit donations. You may even have tried some of these proven strategies before, or simply be curious about others. If an established strategy didn't yield the results you hoped for, don't write it off just yet. Keep reading to find out the exact formula behind it. Odds are, there was a step you weren't aware of, or didn't fully execute. Once you get that missing piece into place, it will make all the difference.

4

STRATEGY #1: THE PARTNERSHIP

> "We make a living by what we get, but we make a life by what we give."
>
> — WINSTON CHURCHILL

While collaboration and partnership has long been recognized as catalysts for success, perhaps no words illustrate the power of collaboration and partnership better than the ancient proverb that says "If you want to go fast, go alone; if you want to go far, go together." As anyone who's taken on a complex endeavor knows, having the right partnership is essential to the outcome of the project.

It's likely you already know what I'm talking about. If you've been lucky, you might have experienced the incredible power that results from working with the right person or organization. But there is also a chance you've drowned in work you could have avoided had you collaborated with others or have felt the deep frustration of dealing with the wrong type of people for your project.

Regardless of your past experiences, this chapter will guide you on how to unlock the true potential of partnerships. As with all strategies in this book, remember that no one size fits all. Your organization may team up with one key partner or cultivate a network of aligned partnerships to address different needs. Some partnerships might run for a set amount of time, while others may be open-ended.

In this chapter, you'll discover various types of partnerships and learn how to find the perfect fit for you and your organization. You'll also gain insights into building mutually beneficial and enduring partnerships, as well as crafting persuasive partnership pitches for the best odds of success.

THE BENEFITS OF PARTNERSHIPS AND COLLABORATIONS FOR NONPROFITS

Partnership and collaboration can help your nonprofit advance its mission, providing both financial and nonfinancial stability and expanding what you previously saw as possible and attainable.

Though each nonprofit will have its own set of reasons for collaborating with other organizations and individuals, some shared benefits will apply to most.

- **Visibility through cross-promotion:**

By collaborating, you gain access to your partner's network and vice versa. Being featured on their website, social media channels, intranet, and newsletters means you will gain exposure to a fresh audience, generating new interest in your activities and programs.

- **Enhanced goodwill:**

Whatever trust your partner already holds in the eyes of its internal and external audiences, your nonprofit will benefit from it as well. The announcement of a partnership can even serve as an appealing hook for media outlets.

- **Credibility boost:**

Partnering with a well-established brand can significantly boost your organization's credibility. Newer and smaller nonprofits will want to leverage this partnership to build a reputation faster than they would on their own, as it lends credence to their efforts.

- **Strength in numbers:**

Smaller nonprofits often struggle to be heard and make an impact. However, odds are other charities out there are working in the same or adjacent specialties as yours. By banding together with like-minded organizations, you create an opportunity to amplify your collective message. The more organizations you unite with, the louder your advocacy voices will ring, ultimately increasing your impact in the community.

- **Mutual accountability:**

Running a nonprofit can be hard. However, when everyone buys in and gets involved, there is more accountability to drive lasting change.

- **Fresh ideas:**

Inviting new people with diverse experiences, perspectives, and backgrounds to the table infuses your organization with fresh fundraising concepts, opening the door to novel ideas and solutions.

- **Unexpected synergies:**

The possibilities here are endless. You might discover a prime referral opportunity—i.e., your nonprofit serves the unhoused, while your partner offers a job training program. You could direct constituents to them for additional support and vice versa or combine existing programs for increased effectiveness.

- **Cost saving:**

Partnering allows you to save on administrative and operational costs. You can share supplies and workspace, or access better pricing for products and services by pooling resources with your partner.

- **Grant funding:**

Building relationships with like-minded nonprofits can make your application stand out amidst fierce competition. In a study of grant-making foundations, 69 percent actively encouraged collaboration among grantees and 42 percent of these said they sometimes required partnering as a condition for awarding funding (Ostrower, 2005). Moreover, not all sources of funding are open to all, and forging strategic connections opens doors to more opportunities.

EXPLORING DIFFERENT TYPES OF PARTNERSHIPS

Don't limit yourself when thinking of potential partnerships. Most of us will aim for the big brand names (and budgets) but these can be hard to access, and there could be greater benefits from joining forces with a small likeminded organization that shares common stakeholders.

Here are some ideas for you to explore:

1. Corporate partnerships:

Large companies often have generous budgets and may be able to contribute significant amounts to your cause. However, they also receive many requests for support, so standing out from the crowd, especially if your organization is lesser known or on the smaller side, may be a challenge.

2. Small businesses:

Local or regional businesses usually face fewer requests of this type, so competition is less intense. But the benefits of this type of partnership surpass the potential for easier access. Whether the business is a retailer, restaurant, or service provider, partnering with a small business in your area means that you will most likely share a similar niche, as you both have an interest in serving the same community or population.

3. Influencers:

Have you ever logged on to social media and been influenced to click on something or donate to a cause because someone you follow suggested it? If so, then you are already aware of the power of influencers. As with businesses, bigger is not always better. Micro-influencers, with followings from anything between 10k and 100k followers, might be easier to access and could resonate better with your niche.

4. Media organizations:

Local newspapers or TV stations can be invaluable allies. Provide them with compelling content that champions your cause so they can amplify your message to a wider audience.

5. Other organizations:

Government agencies, community organizations, or even associations and coalitions (such as those targeted at certain professions, or certain causes, like economic development) can also make good partners. Think broadly. For example, if your mission relates to improving literacy, a library could be a naturally aligned partner.

HOW CAN YOUR PARTNER SUPPORT YOUR NONPROFIT?

Say you've already scored a meeting with a potential partner for your organization. Right off the bat, they'll want to know what the partnership will entail and what you are asking of them. Don't arrive to the meeting waiting for their suggestions: show them a well-defined route and plan so they don't feel overwhelmed by additional work.

Consider the following ideas:

Direct donations are the most straightforward route. These could be cash, in-kind donations, or a combination of both. In-kind contributions can be physical items like food or equipment, or they can be intangible, such as with time and labor support. For example, you might receive pro bono advice on marketing or legal issues. You can also explore joint venture campaigns, where partners collaborate on fundraising initiatives. If partnering with a local coffee shop, for example, they set up a station to help collect donations for the fundraiser or round up their purchase to the next dollar.

Workplace giving is a growing channel that taps into a company's workforce. Companies can encourage staff to donate to charity and make it convenient by directly deducting a set amount from their paychecks. Large companies may even match employee donations, serving as a strong incentive for giving. Roughly $2–$3 billion is donated through matching gift programs every year, and a third of donors would give more if it would be matched (Double the Donation, 2022). Workplace giving can take place during a specific time-limited campaign or year-round. According to America's Charities, around $5 billion is raised through workplace giving annually. Establishing a payroll deduction with an established company can create a reliable income stream for a nonprofit.

Volunteering schemes can also give your nonprofit access to extra helping hands. You can use volunteers to help at events or help with behind-the-scenes operational work. There is, however, a caveat: When designing volunteering schemes, make sure you are not accidentally increasing your workload or assigning them tasks that will become frustrating. By aligning their skills with your needs, you increase the likelihood of future volunteering from them.

WHAT CAN YOUR NONPROFIT OFFER?

Remember, partnerships are mutually beneficial. So far we've talked about the ways your nonprofit can benefit from working with a different organization, but you should also have a clear idea of what you can offer to potential allies.

Partnering with a trusted nonprofit can improve how customers or clients view a company or organization. There's evidence to back this up: according to America's Charities, 90% of businesses indicate that partnering with reputable nonprofits enhances their brand. Through partnership, you can help them build a reputation within a community, influencing people to choose their products or services, thus driving sales or loyalty.

The benefit of cross-promotion also goes both ways. A corporate partner or sponsor can expect to receive prominent advertising opportunities in return for the partnership. Corporate partners or sponsors will often expect prominent advertising opportunities in return for their partnership. Display their name and logo on your campaign collateral, digital platforms, and other marketing materials to increase their visibility.

Charitable partnerships also tend to improve staff morale, leading to higher productivity and longer employee retention. Working for an employer that contributes to and cares about a good cause creates a source of pride and purpose among employees.

Keep in mind that corporate partners will often ask for data indicating the impact of their contribution. Document the benefits of the partnership both qualitatively and quantitatively. This can help foster long-lasting relationships.

Remember: Having a clear sense of what you can offer as part of a partnership is essential to getting the attention of potential partners and retaining them in productive, harmonious relationships.

10 STEPS TO SECURING QUALITY PARTNERSHIPS

Creating great partnerships for your nonprofit doesn't have to be complicated. Follow these steps to identify, approach, and secure partners, and ensure a healthy and beneficial ongoing relationship for both sides.

1. Start with a mission statement:

Your nonprofit should have a guiding mission statement that defines your goals. Whatever your North Star, use it when wading into partnership waters. Use it to identify potential partners who align with your purpose and can help you achieve your mission without distorting your message.

Example: If your nonprofit focuses on environmental conservation, look for partners that share a commitment to sustainability and ecological preservation.

2. Identify potential partners within your network:

Start by exploring close connections within your current network, including staff, advocates, and loyal donors. You can utilize their professional and personal connections to make introductions to key contacts.

Look for reputable companies with a community presence. Seek out companies that have a link to presence in your community. They could be exclusively local or be a larger organization with a branch in the area. Consider organizations that naturally align with your nonprofit's mission and could make ideal partners.

Example: An animal rescue organization could partner with a local pet store or a food bank with a nearby supermarket.

3. Find common ground:

The most successful partnerships share a purpose, audience, vision, or values. Identify where your views align with potential partners and brainstorm how a collaboration could deliver impact, benefits, or efficiencies.

Example: If your nonprofit focuses on youth empowerment, partner with an organization that shares a similar goal to provide mentorship or job opportunities for young people.

4. Ensure compatibility:

On that note, it's essential to emphasize the need for shared values. An oil company would not make a logical partner for an environmental nonprofit. Look for partners with aligned brands, missions, and cultures. No amount of money is worth a partnership that you wouldn't be proud to promote.

Example: An outdoor and sporting goods store would likely be a fantastic partner for an environmental nonprofit, as their customers likely have an interest in preserving the environment.

5. Present your vision and objectives compellingly:

Be clear about the needs of your nonprofit and express your aspirations for the future. Be clear about what it takes to run your projects and programs. If it requires a certain amount to ensure the viability of these each year, be upfront about that. Share key metrics, outcomes, and compelling narratives that illustrate the impact of your work, particularly if working with a previously existing partner. Humans are naturally driven by storytelling; make the most of that. You can then shift into articulating your request and what you have to offer in exchange.

Example: Share stories of individuals or communities who have benefited from your nonprofit and explain how additional resources could amplify your impact. You can even record testimonials of your beneficiaries so your partner or potential partner can put a face and voice to the data.

6. Show what you can bring to the table:

Highlight what your nonprofit can offer and how it can solve a problem or provide value to your potential partner. Clearly articulate the benefits and impact they can expect from the partnership. Look for the win-win. Even if it seems obvious, spell out exactly what's in it for the other party. This is especially relevant if they haven't engaged in similar partnerships in the past.

Engage in open discussions and listen to their goals. Get to know what impact or success would look like for them, how they prefer to engage with communities, and what aspects of your cause interest them.

Involve them in the development of the partnership engagement before actually moving into any solicitation. They may have useful ideas to contribute and getting early buy-in is the first step to a commitment. Leave space and time for discussion and further consideration: identifying a point person for communication will keep things moving along.

Example: If you run a food-focused nonprofit, highlight how you can make use of surplus food items from their business, reducing waste, and benefiting the local community.

7. Determine the details of the partnership and align expectations:

Agree on the level of donation, sponsorship, or volunteering that both parties find valuable. Clearly define each partner's role and responsibilities, as well as the intended outcomes of the partnership.

Example: Create a memorandum of understanding or contract that outlines the contributions and expectations of each partner.

8. Set up strategy meetings and execute the plan:

Collaborate on fundraising initiatives or events that benefit both parties. Get specific about deliverables, such as promotional opportunities and social media mentions.

Example: Don't leave things up in the air or assume you are on the same page without addressing it first. Where will you display their name and logo, and vice versa? Will you put out a press release? Who will distribute it? How often or how many times will you mention your partner on social media or in newsletters? What would success look like?

9. Get the campaign rolling:

Once you've found a suitable partner, finalized the details, and are ready to launch your campaign or event, it's important to assign tasks to each person involved. This lets each individual focus on a specific effort and leverage their unique talents and skills.

Example: Partnerships can take diverse compositions, but everyone should have a crucial role to fill. This can range from finding prospective donors and nurturing relationships with them to soliciting donations, recognizing contributors, engaging in community advocacy, managing media engagement, and conducting marketing and promotion through various channels.

10. Keep collaboration harmonious and productive:

Maintaining clear, open communication is the cornerstone of a great partnership. Remember to regularly step back and assess how things are going. Seek feedback and suggestions from your partner. Track the progress of your shared initiatives and the return on investment.

Example: Ask yourself the following questions and return to them periodically:

1. Are we delivering the solution we originally envisioned?
2. What has been the impact of our work so far, and how has it been received?
3. How can we effectively measure and collect data to assess our progress?
4. In which areas can we make improvements?
5. What aspects of our partnership are performing well?
6. What larger macro trends are currently shaping the landscape, and how should we factor them into our plans?
7. Do all partners feel empowered to contribute their insights and fulfill their roles effectively?

SUMMARY

Partnerships, whether with fellow nonprofits, corporations, small businesses, or influencers, play a crucial role in helping your nonprofit create a broader impact and expand its reach. Strong partnerships can emerge from unexpected sources, often within your existing network or community. The more you understand and learn about your closest connections, the better the odds of tapping into a great potential partner.

Get a sense for what sponsors look to gain from a nonprofit partnership. Partnering with a charity benefits their interests as well. This understanding will assist you in crafting a mutually beneficial proposal. Focus on long-term transformation rather than short-term transactions.

Once you've identified promising partnership opportunities, be sure to nurture a relationship. Great partnerships are built on shared interests and thrive on consistent and effective communication. Regularly evaluate the partnership to ensure it continues to deliver value to all parties involved.

Our next fundraising strategy focuses on leveraging donors. When you're ready, let's delve into understanding their desires and motivations, so you can establish stronger connections, foster mutually beneficial relationships, and explore various approaches to attract new supporters for your fundraiser.

5

STRATEGY #2: BRINGING IN DONORS

Ever wondered what really motivates your top donors? Take a moment to step into their shoes and see things from their perspective. Understanding the mindset of a donor is a skill that every nonprofit professional should master. Believe it or not, supporters contribute for a multitude of reasons that go way beyond just the tax perks. It could be a personal connection to your mission that ignites their passion, the thrill of being part of a movement greater than themselves, or the desire to make a positive impact with their hard-earned dollars. Plus, donating to charities simply feels good. It's been scientifically proven that acts of generosity release dopamine, so we literally get a happiness boost from helping others.

According to a survey by Network for Good (2018), the top motivator among donors was being mission-driven. They're drawn to your organization because of its mission, but they stay when you consistently demonstrate commitment, reliability, and transparency. Being true to your word and acting consistently is the way to earn their trust. On the flip side, a lack of accountability is the main reason donors pull back their support.

Ultimately, what matters to most donors is impact. They want to see tangible evidence that shows them how their money is being used to help others in the world. When they know their money has been put to good use, they feel a sense of empowerment and like they're part of something bigger than themselves.

This chapter will help you delve into the complex world of donors to understand their motivations and desires and gain insights into how to create long-lasting and beneficial relationships with them.

Some donors are natural do-gooders, driven by an inherent altruism. It's their way of making a moral difference. Others have a personal connection to a cause and can often turn out to be your most passionate and loyal advocates. And a different group might be mostly interested in the financial incentives for making charitable contributions. Most donors can access a tax deduction, depending on the status of the organization they're supporting. And, evidently, these groups are not mutually exclusive and can often overlap.

Whatever their motivations, understanding your donors and creating strong relationships with them can truly make magic happen. Let's get to it.

WHY ARE DONORS SO IMPORTANT?

Why are donors so crucial in the world of fundraising? If you are reading this book, chances are you might already know or at least have a sense of the answer to this question. Still, donors are so important it's worth digging into the details.

First and foremost, donors bring in the funds that keep your organization running. Without them, it's tough to keep the lights on. Among them, loyal donors are the real gems and the ones worth fighting for. Their regular donations provide a consistent and reliable source of income—no more anxiously waiting for the next influx of money. When you can predict a certain amount of income each month or quarter, you can plan more effectively and focus your time and energy on your operational activities.

But that's hardly it. Donors also play a vital role in boosting your message, generating greater awareness, and funding. Technology has made it possible to encourage donors to easily spread the word by sharing their support online, reaching even more people. And let's not forget the personal touch. Never underestimate the power of a simple request to tell friends and family about your fundraiser. Even if only a fraction of a donor's network—family, friends, neighbors, acquaintances, and colleagues—are introduced to your organization, your organization can reach far beyond its usual borders. Finally, donors can bring new ideas into your organization. Sometimes, it takes an external perspective to spot opportunities for innovation and improvement. Those fresh eyes and fresh perspectives might be just what your organization needs from time to time. Donor relationships can also open doors to other exciting opportunities, such as corporate sponsorships and major donors. Don't underestimate the power of individuals and the potential connections they may have or the combined efforts they can make. Who knows what they could offer to support your cause?

THE IMPORTANCE OF LOYAL DONORS

I want to take a moment to explain the importance of long-term, committed donors and why they are worth the investment over one-off donations.

Regular donors demonstrate a remarkable commitment by giving significantly more compared to their one-time counterparts—an astounding 440 percent more, to be exact. Although recurring donations might have a lower individual value than single contributions, the power of consistent support far outweighs this difference. In fact, studies have shown that the average lifetime financial return from a recurring donor is just over $795, while that of a one-time donor amounts to only $147 (Philanthropy News Digest, 2018).

Moreover, acquiring new donors can be extremely costly —there is recruiting, training, managing fundraisers, and extensive marketing efforts. These expenses often surpass the cost of retaining your current supporters. Existing donors will always give your nonprofit the most bang for the buck. Every time you start from scratch with a new donor, you have to educate them about your work and build trust from the ground up. While donor acquisition should always be a priority, don't forget your current supporter base. Remember, one size does not fit all—take into account each individual's giving history when cultivating and maintaining donor relationships.

Think about long-term donors as friendships. Like the best relationships, they take time and effort to cultivate, but also yield the most rewarding outcomes—ones that can last a lifetime.

THE 6 MAIN TYPES OF DONORS

Donors can come from anywhere and take all shapes and forms. They will all have different reasons for giving, as well as different ways to do so. For the purpose of this chapter, let's break them down into six main categories:

1. Individual Donors:

These are the most common donors and, collectively, will form the core of your supporter base. While gaining or losing one here or there won't make a noticeable difference, they can add up to account for a significant chunk of your nonprofit's income. Once you secure a new individual donor and they make a gift to your organization, celebrate them and be sure of keeping in touch. Follow up with a personal thank you and explain how their gift will be used, and share information on upcoming events, initiatives, or programs.

2. Major Donors:

Major donors aren't secured in one fell swoop; they are frequently the result of years of sustained effort. Cultivating major donors takes time and effort, but it's worth it because of the large sums they can provide. Depending on the size, major gifts can change the trajectory of your organization. If you have the staff, select someone to work with major donors, conduct research, build profiles, nurture the relationship, and steward communications over the long run.

Unlike organizational or corporate donors, major donors have the freedom to give without committee consultations or sign-offs. This makes them an ideal choice if your nonprofit has an urgent, specific need. If a project truly resonates with them, they might even fund the entire initiative. Treat major donors as VIPs and remember that each donor is a unique individual and more than just a wallet. Connect with them on a personal level above all else. Major donors don't need a hard sell but will want to be kept up to date. Like any other donor, seeing the impact of their gift is powerful.

3. Corporate donors:

As for-profit businesses, corporate donors will require an exchange of value to secure their support. Typically, they will expect to receive advertising and publicity for their brand in return for their contribution. This could be as simple as promotion through your nonprofit's own marketing channels, or at the other end of the scale, having naming rights to a building or facility. That being said, some CEOs or senior leaders may have personal passions for specific causes. Leverage that motivator.

Regardless, corporate social responsibility is now a top priority, and businesses are expected to contribute to the communities they operate in—so it's worth considering how corporate donors fit into your fundraising strategy.

4. Foundations:

These institutions are often the unsung heroes of philanthropy. Candid (2020) reveals that there are over 100,000 foundations in the US, with over $80 billion to give out. They usually award grants only in certain key focus areas: mostly health and education, as well as those affected by economic disadvantages, including children and youth.

When dealing with foundations, remember that accountability is key. Grant recipients often have the responsibility to demonstrate measurable outcomes, ensuring that the foundation's investment yields tangible results. Although grants for capital or operating expenses are less common, the potential for financial support remains significant.[1] Remember that foundations themselves operate as nonprofits. Community foundations generate funds directly from the public, while corporations may establish foundations as separate legal entities. Additionally, private foundations, like the Bill & Melinda Gates Foundation emerge from the passion of individuals or families, carrying out their own impactful programs. Be sure to align your organization's mission with the foundations you approach.

5. Organizations:

While organizations are a lesser-known source of funding, they certainly deserve a starring role in your donor strategy. Trade or professional associations, coalitions, sports clubs, and even churches can emerge as unexpected champions. Cast your net far and wide and don't overlook community organizations.

6. Volunteers and advocates:

These passionate individuals are a valuable category of donor in their own right and hold a special place in the donor realm. For some, giving time rather than money is the best way for them to contribute, though this may evolve—depending on their personal circumstances.

The young and spirited often have an abundance of spare time and passion and may one day become a financial donor as their situation changes. Older people on fixed incomes might not just have free time but may even leave a lasting legacy through a bequest. Some of your volunteers may be volunteering mainly in order to gain credits or fulfill some type of requirement for work or school. If this is the case, you can play up this angle in your content and marketing to attract more similar volunteers. Remember, recognition is key. Acknowledge their participation and commitment. When volunteers feel appreciated, they can become the driving force that keeps on giving and helps recruit others as well.

HOW TO BRING IN DONORS FOR A FUNDRAISER

You already know the different types of donors out there and why they are so important to your nonprofit. So you may now be wondering: How do I bring them in? Finding new donors and getting their attention (and money) can be a frustrating experience: competition is fierce among nonprofits and donors' capabilities might be limited.

But you don't need to lose sleep over this. Let's break down the best ways to do it.

Start by identifying your main objective and mapping out your fundraising strategy (refer to Chapter 3). Ensure your messaging is donor-centric, appealing to what they care about and emphasizing the impact and outcomes of their giving. Your appeal should speak to their hearts, not just their heads. Remember that stories resonate most with people, so incorporate personal anecdotes and humanize your mission. Along with numbers and graphs, be sure to put a human face to your work, personalizing and humanizing the work you do.

Once you've developed your appeal, it's time to promote it. Consider your audience's preferences and determine the most effective channels for reaching and engaging with them. Begin soliciting donors through your chosen mediums.

Get your website ready to attract donors. Choose powerful images that showcase the people benefiting from your work. Don't forget to share touching stories and videos that truly demonstrate your impact. When you talk to your readers, speak directly to them, like you're having a conversation. Remember, you are appealing to their hearts. You could invite them to "learn about Alex's incredible fight for life" or "discover how your support is making a real difference in regenerating rainforests." You could even add some features to display the support you are receiving, showing recent donations in a dynamic feed or a friendly alert that says something like, "Hey, guess what? Riley from California just donated $50, which means 5 children in Benin will get brand-new shoes!" See the pattern? Frame the donor as the hero of the story; honestly, it's their contributions that make all the difference.

Since we are talking about your website, make sure your donation buttons grab attention. Go for bold colors and compelling calls to action such as: "Feed a child today," "Save the endangered black rhino," or "Send essential supplies to people fleeing their homes." Don't be afraid to try something extra, like a pop-up box alongside your donation buttons. Yes, it can seem intrusive, but every person who visits your website with the intention of donating will be grateful. Test it and see how it works for you.

Simplify those donation forms. Stick to the essentials: name, contact info, and payment details. The smoother and quicker the process, the higher the chances people will complete them. Don't forget to test them on mobile devices, as many people will be accessing your forms on a phone or tablet. Make sure to include a link to your donation page in all your communications. It's all about making it as easy as possible for people to contribute.

Make sure your emails are action-packed. Include multiple opportunities to take action, like donation buttons and attention-grabbing links. Many of us are subscribed to too many newsletters, so make sure yours are entertaining. Segment your email list so you can tailor your messages: you wouldn't send the same email to a fresh-faced donor as you would to a long-time supporter. Set up an automated welcome email that introduces new subscribers to your nonprofit's story and mission. Show them the impact of your work right from the start.

Don't just depend on social media and don't expect donations to come rolling in as soon as you hit publish on a post. Social media is often more of an awareness tool than a conversion one. Think about the importance of one-on-one. Consider incorporating phone outreach into your donor campaign. Depending on your team's resources, you can make individual calls or even organize a phone-a-thon. Speaking directly to donors over the phone gives you a valuable opportunity to explain how their gift makes a difference. Develop a base script for callers to ensure consistency and success. And don't shrug the power of merchandise. From mugs to keychains or tea towels, they are a fun way to get your message or brand to cut through the noise and get new donors interested. Make sure to include social media handles somewhere in there to make it easier for them to get in touch.

Make the most of your existing supporter base. Reach out to your loyal advocates, including board members, volunteers, and donors, and ask them to help spread the word. They're invested in your success, and sharing your cause with others is an uncomplicated and effective way for them to support you. Additionally, reconnect with previous donors. Just because someone hasn't donated in a while doesn't mean they've lost interest. It's possible that your nonprofit simply slipped off their radar, and they may even appreciate hearing from you. Don't hesitate to reach out and acknowledge their past support. One-time or lapsed donors are still potential supporters. Personalize your message as much as possible, mentioning their previous contribution amount, date, and how it made an impact.

Take the time to research and connect with promising prospects. Begin by reviewing your internal database and identifying those who have shown a likelihood to donate based on specific factors. Look into annual reports and newsletters from similar organizations to discover their key donors. (More on handling major donors coming up soon.) Extend your reach even further through collaborations with aligned organizations. Their audiences may be like minds who become your supporters as well. Refer back to Chapter 4 on building strategic partnerships or sponsorships.

Search for major donors. They make significant contributions and play a vital role in sustaining your funding. Start by identifying your most generous existing donors if you don't have a major donor portfolio. Who has given the largest sums? Screen your database and learn from your top donors. Then, do some prospect research to find others who might be inclined to give in a comparable and equivalent way. Once you scout out and identify optimal prospective major donors, develop a personalized outreach strategy. Building a connection and understanding their priorities and motivators is crucial. While you know they have the capacity to give, persuading them to take that leap requires a compelling case. Major gifts aren't randomly given; they stem from a profound connection between an individual and a cause.

SUMMARY

It might seem like common sense, but it's worth reiterating: donors are the lifeblood of your nonprofit. They are essential for your organization's survival and the impact you make in people's lives. Understanding your supporter base, which can include individuals, major donors, corporations, foundations, organizations, and volunteers, is key. By knowing their motivations, you can tailor your campaign messaging to truly cater to their needs, finding your way into their hearts and wallets.

Don't be afraid to make bold requests, asking for their support in amplifying your message and mission. With a solid foundation of credibility and trust, many supporters will gladly step up as ambassadors and advocates.

Before moving on, think about your existing and potential donors. How can you improve communication with them? Are you reaching all your potential supporters, or have you settled in a comfort zone? And how can you turn your current one-off donations into sustained ones? Ask yourself these questions and think of ways in which you can put everything you've learned through this chapter into action.

We will now dive into the world of social media. While it's a rapidly changing landscape, there are timeless fundraising principles that apply across different platforms. By executing effectively and leveraging each channel, you can navigate any algorithm updates and maximize your online presence.

6

STRATEGY #3: THE DIGITAL FUNDRAISER

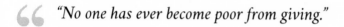 *"No one has ever become poor from giving."*

— MAYA ANGELOU

Social media has revolutionized countless industries, and the charitable sector is no exception. Gone are the days of relying solely on traditional media or partners to boost your publicity efforts. With social media, you now have the opportunity to have unprecedented control over your brand and messaging. Social platforms offer nonprofits a direct route to reach the public, allowing them to share their stories quickly, cost-effectively, and with great impact. They provide a unique opportunity to engage supporters, promote campaigns, and amplify your organization's message.

Consider this: a quarter of donors discover new nonprofits through mobile devices, while up to 55% of people who engage with a nonprofit on social media take meaningful action as a result (Nonprofit Source, 2022). The numbers don't lie: if you hope to organize a successful fundraiser and bring in new donors, then you can't overlook social media.

In this chapter, I will delve into the importance of social media in fundraising and explore how you can effectively harness different platforms for your charitable cause. When we refer to social media, we are talking about websites and applications that allow us to post, share, and engage with content. These platforms go beyond mere content consumption; they foster communication and community building. Among the most widely used social media networks, we have Facebook, YouTube, WhatsApp, Instagram, WeChat, and TikTok (Statista, 2022). In the ever-shifting landscape of technology, being on top of your social media game is nonnegotiable. While it can feel overwhelming, the guidelines and best practices I will provide in this chapter will help you navigate this essential arena.

THE ROLE OF SOCIAL MEDIA IN FUNDRAISING

Social media is an essential tool that has transformed the nonprofit sector, particularly in connecting with donors and supporters. These platforms enable individuals, organizations, and causes to amplify their messages and mobilize global support for fundraising. Through crowd-funding, peer-to-peer fundraising, and direct appeals, social media provides a dynamic platform for story-telling, community engagement, and donor participation. It has become an indispensable resource for making a meaningful impact in fundraising efforts.

Your organization is now able to reach more people than ever before. By mastering the art of creating engaging content, your brand can connect with users worldwide. Social networks thrive on content consumption and sharing, with individuals constantly reposting and sending links to their networks. Algorithms recognize engagement and amplify the reach of well-received content. By actively participating and being present, you increase your chances of being discovered. This, in turn, makes it easier to inspire your followers to take concrete actions, whether it's calling politicians, attending protests, or making personal changes. Even someone across the globe can contribute to your fundraiser with a simple click or sign a petition.

Unleash the power of storytelling to propel your brand awareness forward. By sharing the compelling narratives of your organization and its cause, you can ignite a sense of connection and empathy among your audience.

Illuminate the personal stories of individuals whose lives have been positively transformed by your work and showcase the real impact you make. Through the art of storytelling, you have the ability to captivate hearts and inspire action. Share the driving force behind your nonprofit's inception, what motivates your current staff and volunteers, and how your fundraisers and programs have positively impacted the lives of those you serve. Show your donors that their support is valued and demonstrate the difference they make. Regular posts and updates will help you maintain a strong connection with them, fostering a sense of community even when you are countries apart.

Finally, these media platforms have made communication two-way. Rather than reading an advertisement in a magazine or staring at a TV screen, users can now voice their opinion and interest in various topics, allowing organizations to tap directly into their interests and concerns. This is known as social media monitoring or social listening, an approach that can help you refine your online communication. By paying attention to what individuals are already saying about relevant subjects, you gain valuable insights into how your nonprofit is perceived and what information your audience seeks. Monitoring direct mentions of your organization and campaigns is essential, but it is equally important to keep tabs on popular issues among your audience and the discussions among top influencers. With these insights, you can adjust fundraising messaging, target digital ads based on demographics or interests, and effectively engage your audience.

DIGITAL PLATFORMS FOR FUNDRAISING

While the social media landscape is ever-changing, it's worth knowing the most important platforms at the moment. Keep in mind, not every social media app might be the one for your nonprofit. Choosing the right one for you will depend on a number of different factors: whether your content is mostly text-based or visual; if you have a dedicated AV team; and the amount of content you can generate. Keep reading to learn more about the most important social media platforms right now and how to choose the right one for your organization.

Facebook's sheer size is obviously its biggest drawback, but the other benefits for nonprofits are the cherry on top. You can add a donation button to your charity's Facebook page, create custom stickers for Stories or even hold a real-time fundraising drive via Facebook Live. Since it's owned by the same company that owns Instagram, both platforms can be integrated to facilitate your work. Keep in mind, however, that Facebook's user base is now slightly older. If your nonprofit appeals to younger audiences, it might be worthwhile considering some of the more visual platforms on this list.

Twitter is a fast-moving social media network that's particularly useful for breaking news and jumping on the day's trending topics. It is often favored by influential users in media, technology, and politics, so it can be an incredibly useful platform to connect with relevant figures in various fields. Use Twitter to advocate for your cause, engage in current events, and connect with other experts of organizations in the same niche. Twitter might be a great platform for your nonprofit if you are vocal and engage in current debates.

Instagram is particularly useful for nonprofits with visually compelling content. Nonprofits capable of generating impactful and captivating images and videos will thrive here. Organizations can leverage features like Instagram Stories, IGTV, and Reels to showcase behind-the-scenes footage, highlight success stories, and provide valuable educational content. The platform also offers the chance to add a donation button and to drive direct support from followers. As I mentioned, Instagram and Facebook can be integrated quite seamlessly.

TikTok is a fairly new addition to the social media scene but has soared in popularity quickly. Its TikTok for Good program offers account management help to nonprofits, along with advanced analytics and promoted hashtags.

TikTok's user base is quite young so it might not be the best platform if you are looking to find new donors, though it could be quite useful for recruiting volunteers. Keep in mind that TikTok is all about short videos and live streams, so you will need to tailor your message to this format.

YouTube is just as much a search-based platform as it is a social media platform. This platform is great for sharing longer videos, tutorials, or how-to videos, and live streams. This content can include testimonials, success stories, behind-the-scenes footage, and educational videos. By consistently uploading high-quality videos, optimizing them with relevant keywords and tags, and sharing them across social media channels, your organization can create a thriving and engaged community.

Reddit is an extremely popular forum with a substantial user base that skews toward mostly a young and predominantly male audience. While overt self-promotion is generally discouraged, nonprofits can establish meaningful connections through authentic engagement and by hosting Ask Me Anything (AMA) sessions. These interactive sessions provide an opportunity for organizations to answer questions, share insights, and build rapport with their community. Be aware, however, that most Reddit users are anonymous, which can generate trolling.

Pinterest serves as a visually appealing platform that serves as a digital scrapbook and has a predominantly young to middle-aged female user base. It allows users to save content from your website and is particularly suitable for organizations operating in the arts or nature/conservation sectors, as it offers an ideal medium to showcase captivating photos, engaging videos, and informative infographics. You can also use Pinterest to promote merchandise and product sales as part of your fundraising efforts, especially if you can position them as gift ideas for key occasions like holidays or other seasonal events.

SOCIAL MEDIA ADVERTISING

Now that you know the main social media platforms for nonprofits, let's dive into the game-changing world of social media advertising. With a flood of content being created every minute, it's becoming increasingly challenging to stand out from the crowd. This is where paid promotion comes in. Each social network offers ways for brands to boost their content and reach a wider audience. You can target specific audiences and optimize your campaigns for different outcomes, whether it's reaching as many people as possible or maximizing donations. Start small, test, learn, and then scale up your efforts. Remember that algorithms are constantly changing, so mastering the art of social media advertising requires constant tinkering.

Make sure your website is ready to track the traffic and actions generated by your campaigns. Tools like Google Analytics are easy to use and can provide extremely valuable information. Don't overlook micro conversions like video views or visits to your donation form—they can be valuable interactions. And of course, don't forget about macro conversions like donations, newsletter registrations, and event signups. This will all provide valuable information on how to spend your money on advertising.

Think beyond social media and consider advertising through Google as well. Google Grants funding offers nonprofits $10,000 in free ad spending every month. With the average cost per click for advocacy ads being around $1.50, this could drive a significant amount of traffic to your website, potentially resulting in valuable donations. The process to qualify for Google Grants is not automatic, however, so you will need to apply and meet criteria, which exclude certain nonprofits like schools and educational institutions, government organizations, and healthcare organizations.

DIGITAL FUNDRAISING

Social media and other digital tools are not just great for communication and fostering community, but for fundraising, streamlining the donation process. and allowing you to reach potential donors like never before.

Your nonprofit's website is a crucial player in your digital fundraising efforts, so it's essential to optimize it for donation collection. Add strategically placed calls-to-action and donation buttons in prominent spots throughout your site and streamline your campaign landing pages and donation forms to make the giving process as simple as possible. Consider implementing payment pop-up boxes to enhance giving, and experiment with different visuals and copy to analyze which combinations yield the best results. Don't forget to thoroughly test your website on mobile devices as well as desktops: half of your traffic will come from mobile devices (Double the Donation, 2022). So if your website and its donation buttons perform poorly on mobile, you're missing out on valuable interactions.

Email marketing will be another key pillar in your digital fundraising strategy. Leverage your email list as a valuable asset. A good email marketing platform, even if not specifically designed for nonprofits, allows you to segment your audience based on tags like location, income, interests, and giving level, enabling customized communications. It should also offer scheduling features. Check at what time your email list is most likely to click on links or open the email to optimize your mailing times.

When crafting fundraising emails, put effort into creating compelling subject lines that are both descriptive/evocative and action-oriented. Emojis can boost open rates, and personalizing emails with recipients' names adds a personal touch. Remember that emails often display a preview snippet, so make it captivating to pique curiosity. In the body of the email, get straight to the point and make your first request within the first couple of paragraphs. Include multiple calls to action throughout the email, using different phrasing or display styles like links or buttons. However, keep it focused—direct all calls to action to the same place. Avoid overwhelming recipients by asking them to donate, RSVP to an event, and register as a volunteer all in one email.

You can also take your digital fundraising offline by using quick response (QR) codes, which you can add to merchandising and offline advertising. These black and white squares have a unique pattern that can be scanned using the phone's camera app to direct users to specific digital destinations, such as websites or PDFs. Countless websites will allow you to create a unique QR code: you just need to provide your destination link.

Finally, crowdfunding is an increasingly popular tactic in digital fundraising. As mentioned in a previous chapter, crowdfunding harnesses the power of social media, crowdsourcing donations from far and wide to support a campaign. GoFundMe is one of the most well-known crowdfunding platforms, but there are many others well suited to nonprofit fundraisers including:

- **GoFundMe** is the leading crowdfunding platform. With its intuitive and user-friendly interface, it is extremely easy to use even for novices. It features excellent social sharing tools and a secure platform for online donations, with flexible payment options. It also offers features like goal tracking, updates, and donor communication tools to keep campaigners and donors engaged.
- **Crowdfunder** offers the advantage of zero fees and provides dedicated coaches to support your fundraising campaign, along with the opportunity to offer rewards and access donation matching programs.
- **TheGivingMachine** introduces innovative features such as collecting donations through

retail partners and a unique giving lottery scheme.

- **GlobalGiving** not only serves as a fundraising platform but also provides corporate partnerships, match-funding opportunities, and additional tools and training for nonprofits.
- **Givey** is great for smaller charities, particularly those based in the UK.

Take some time to explore the different crowdfunding platforms out there and look for the best one for your organization. With this wide array of crowdfunding platforms at your disposal, you can tap into the support of a global community to fuel your nonprofit's mission.

10 STEPS FOR A SUCCESSFUL DIGITAL FUNDRAISER

1. Define your goals and target audience:

Identify who you want to reach and prioritize the appropriate channels for your fundraising efforts. Follow your ideal donors and tailor your content to their interests and communication patterns.

2. Set up your nonprofit account:

Take advantage of any additional benefits you might have as a nonprofit and ensure your team understands how to maximize the platform's features.

3. Assign clear roles to all team members:

Don't assume someone will be on top of something if you don't previously agree on it. Agree on who will write, design, and publish content. Who will monitor and respond to questions or comments? Who will check your inbox periodically?

4. Create a content calendar:

Plan your posts, considering key dates and events worth leveraging in your campaign. From Mother's Day or International Women's Day to Earth Hour or World Oceans Day, there are endless dates to organize campaigns around.

5. Share compelling stories:

Highlight the people behind your mission, showcase the impact of your nonprofit, and acknowledge the generosity of donors. Make it personal: Instagram photos containing faces are 38% more likely to garner likes and 32% more likely to be commented on than those without faces (Georgia Tech, 2014). Introduce your donors and supporters to what life is like behind the scenes—show them who your staff and volunteers are and what they do. You can also share stories about the donors who have helped your cause. Acknowledge their generosity and the impact it has enabled. Invite them to share in these victories and spread the word.

6. Use visuals and interactive features:

Leverage images, videos, live streams, and interactive features on platforms like Instagram and Facebook to enhance engagement and reach a wider audience. The more interaction your content receives, the higher the chances that the platform will prioritize it for a wider audience.

7. Include clear calls to action:

Encourage followers to engage, donate, volunteer, or share your posts. Every post should have a specific call to action. Don't hesitate to invite them to take meaningful actions such as signing up, donating, or volunteering.

Additionally, empower your staff, volunteers, and partners to create their own posts or reshare your organization's content, further fueling the momentum of your
campaign.

8. Partner with other organizations:

Collaborate with aligned companies or agencies to amplify
your campaign's impact. Seek support from high-profile
supporters or advocates to leverage their influence. Reach
out to other companies or agencies that align and inquire
about joining forces to amplify your campaign. And if you
have any high-profile supporters or advocates who are
well known in their own right, ask if they would be willing
to get involved and lend their influence to your cause.

9. Be responsive and stay current:

Reply promptly to comments and messages from your
followers. Stay up to date with platform trends and new
features to remain relevant and stand out online.

10. Don't forget to use hashtags:

Hashtags are incredibly useful to connect with users that
might not be familiar with your nonprofit. Existing rele-

vant and popular hashtags will allow you to expand the organic reach of your posts. For example, a pet shelter might leverage hashtags like #adoptdontshop #animalrescue #animalrights #animallover, or a campaign for Black History Month might use hashtags like #blackhistorymonth or #blackhistoryfacts.

SUMMARY

Digital platforms have transformed how we communicate, connect, and gather support for a cause. Use social media platforms, paid digital advertising, and crowdfunding platforms to harvest the global power of digital media.

In this chapter, I've introduced you to the key platforms for connecting with your audience, expanding your contacts, and engaging in effective fundraising. There's no need to be overwhelmed: take some time to analyze the different options out there and choose the right ones for you. Not every social media platform will be right for your organization, so recognize your strengths and weaknesses, and focus on the ones that will be most useful to you.

Now that you're aware of the key steps involved in planning and delivering a digital fundraiser, let's move on to explore the world of campaigns. In the next chapter, you will develop a thorough understanding of campaigning and how to engage donors and potential partners through this type of strategy.

7

STRATEGY #4: THE CAMPAIGN

In the realm of marketing, there is a crucial concept known as the buyer's journey, a term that refers to the path that potential customers follow from the early realization of a problem to the ultimate purchase decision. Similarly, within the context of a nonprofit, the donor's journey also starts with awareness. Without knowledge of your nonprofit's existence or the issue it tries to address, how can a potential donor decide to support your cause? Awareness stands as the cornerstone of garnering support and is the essential first step to successful fundraising.

Raising awareness is a crucial step in gaining support, and campaigns play a significant role in achieving this. While it is every communicator's dream to come up with a campaign that sets the stage ablaze and gets people talking (and donating), generating awareness is not often the result of a one-hit wonder; it's rather a captivating journey that requires sustained effort and dedication.

In this chapter, we will delve into the significance of campaigns in raising awareness and funds. By understanding the power of campaigns, you'll be equipped to attract potential donors and partners effectively.

WHAT ARE CAMPAIGNS AND WHY ARE THEY SO IMPORTANT?

In essence, these strategic endeavors are tools used by organizations and individuals to spread public awareness and foster understanding about specific issues, causes, or topics. They can also be implemented to gather economic support or rally volunteers for a cause they are already aware of. But before we delve into the different types of campaigns and how to effectively design and implement one, I want to take a few minutes to highlight their importance. Successful awareness campaigns have the ability to shape our perceptions and behaviors, and chances are you've been influenced by campaigns orchestrated by nonprofits.

Think back to 2014 when buckets of ice were raining down on people's heads—yes, the aforementioned ALS Ice Bucket Challenge. This viral sensation not only raised worldwide awareness but also generated substantial donations for amyotrophic lateral sclerosis (ALS). And if you're a bit older, you might recall the incredible combination of awareness campaigns that led to the history-making Montreal Protocol, an international agreement signed in 1987 to protect the ozone layer by phasing out the production and use of ozone-depleting substances. These examples showcase the transformative power of well-crafted awareness campaigns: not only can they unlock significant financial support for important causes, but also reshape the world.

While your work is ongoing and permanent, campaigns run for a determined time frame, potentially taking on several iterations over time to truly galvanize support. Although it may seem like you're bombarding people with the same message, the truth is that the public often needs repeated exposure for it to truly sink in.

Moreover, designing and executing an awareness campaign will enhance your nonprofit's internal dynamics. They don't just spur your donors into action but help focus your team's efforts and energy on a big vision for the future. The structure of a campaign calls for robust planning and budgeting, reinforcing your nonprofit's internal capacity, including infrastructure, systems, and technology. As your team gains campaign experience, future initiatives will run even more smoothly, harnessing the full potential of your organization.

TYPES OF FUNDRAISING CAMPAIGNS

It's very likely that at any given time, your nonprofit will be either actively campaigning or planning for a campaign. Campaigns come in a variety of shapes and sizes—beyond just raffles, walk-a-thons, or galas—and we'll dive into this diverse landscape now.

As we have already established, building public awareness is a fundamental component of any nonprofit's fundraising strategy. Using **awareness campaigns**, you can educate the public, fostering a deeper connection to the issue at stake. Think, for example, about the Earth Hour Campaign, a global environmental campaign initiated by the World Wildlife Fund (WWF) and designed to raise awareness about climate change and the need for energy conservation, or the It Gets Better Project, which was launched to support LGBTQ+ youth and combat bullying and discrimination. The more people are aware of your cause, the likelier they are to connect to support it.

Online fundraising campaigns are purely digital initiatives that leverage channels such as email, social media, and digital advertising. A digital campaign run solely on social media is referred to as a social media campaign. While they might seem cheaper to implement, as they happen solely in the digital realm, they will often require impactful videos or interactive content, and have an allocated budget to expand its reach. Likewise, an email campaign focuses on leveraging the power of email marketing, potentially incorporating crowdfunding elements to harness the collective power of online networks and secure numerous small donations. Think, for example, about the emails politicians send during elections, asking supporters to contribute through donations. Additionally, individuals can also create their own personal fundraising campaigns, known as peer-to-peer fundraising, tapping into their personal networks to rally support for your cause.

A text-to-give campaign is a simple campaign that enables donors to give to a cause by sending a text message to their cell phone. Keep in mind, potential donors will most likely only engage with a text-to-give campaign if it's around an issue they are already aware of.

Campaigns based around direct marketing tactics, such as door-to-door visits, phone calls, or even direct mail, demand more resources and effort, though the personal touch they offer can make a significant impact.

Membership campaigns focus on converting prospects into donors and increasing contribution levels by building stronger relationships with them. By positioning supporters as members, they feel a greater sense of involvement in the cause, leading to increased loyalty. A supporter who considers themselves a member will feel more involved in a cause and is more likely to give, more often—even if only when their annual membership renewal rolls around.

Capital campaigns are designed to secure major gifts and have the aim of raising a significant sum within a defined timeframe. In most cases, capital campaigns are intended to fund big projects such as renovations or new purchases. For example, your nonprofit might start a crowdfunding campaign to build a school in a foreign country. Typically, these campaigns begin with a quiet phase, during which your team approaches key donors for substantial contributions, which will make up the core funding of your project. This phase tends to require dedicated efforts in research and relationship-building. The subsequent public phase marks the official announcement of the campaign, inviting contributions from a broader audience.

Comprehensive or integrated campaigns can span multiple categories and give people different options to support your organization's diverse needs and be part of something greater. These campaigns can also serve as an opportunity to re-engage with lapsed donors. This type of campaign requires coordination to present a united front to the public. For example, a nonprofit may simultaneously fundraise for a building project and run an annual campaign, allowing major donors to contribute to both initiatives, with the first campaign that reaches out potentially receiving their full support.

9 STEPS TO ORGANIZE SUCCESSFUL FUNDRAISING CAMPAIGNS

Embarking on a successful fundraising campaign requires careful planning and execution. If you're ready to make a difference, follow these essential steps to design and optimize your campaign for success:

1. Choose a campaign type and identify your target audience:

Who does your nonprofit want to reach? Let this knowledge guide your selection of key campaigning channels. If direct mail has brought you success, weave it into your marketing strategy. If digital channels have been your golden ticket, focus your efforts there.

2. Craft a compelling message:

What do you want your audience to know? Design a key message or messages that will shine throughout your campaign. Make it resonate, stay consistent, and speak directly to the hearts of your supporters.

3. Assess your resources and set a budget and timeframe:

Be realistic and strategic. How much can you invest in this campaign, and how much do you aim to raise? Evaluate your resources, plan a fixed campaign budget, and make thoughtful estimates for expenses and revenue. Strike a balance in timing. Give your campaign enough time to gather momentum and attract donations but avoid donor fatigue by not stretching it too long.

4. Measure success with impact:

Identify metrics that will help you gauge the effectiveness of your campaign. How will you measure the impact you're making? Regularly check these metrics and be ready to adjust your strategy along the way if needed.

5. Harness the power of storytelling:

Breathe life into your campaign. Refine your overarching message and craft a succinct narrative that captures attention. Keep your campaign messaging clear and focused. Share impactful stories that put faces to your cause. For instance, meet Nisha, a 12-year-old whose dreams of education are hindered by a lack of access to period care products. Use Nisha's story to show how girls like her are missing out on essential education. Let people see how their donations can change lives and create a brighter future: provide specific examples, such as "just $100 a year will ensure one of her classmates can attend class year-round so she doesn't fall behind on learning." Even more than numbers, personal stories bring a mission to life—showing how someone's life can change. People give to other people, and because of people.

6. Ignite the promotion:

Get people's attention. This is particularly true for digital fundraisers when you want to generate captivating content that reflects the nature of your campaign. It's not business as usual, so ensure your online presence reflects that. Dial up the activity, create buzz, and make it easy to donate. Test your donation process rigorously to ensure a seamless experience. Any glitches at all will lead users to give up and click away. Enable both single and ongoing donations, while reminding the public of the value of recurring donors. If you are working with influencers or encouraging individuals to create their own personal fundraisers, supply them with information and assets so that they represent your nonprofit accurately and consistently.

7. Integrate online and offline elements:

If you have in-person activities, ensure a consistent experience across all touch points. Align messaging and tone across channels. If there are offline elements in your campaign, such as live events, door knocking, etc., ensure all team members are aligned on goals and expectations. A donor who experiences the campaign across different touch points should have a seamless experience that is consistent with the organization they have come to know.

8. Keep the momentum going:

As the campaign nears its end, step up your efforts. As the campaign reaches its end period, it might be tempting to ease off, but this is often the time to step up your efforts. If you are making your fundraising goal public, regularly update how far you are from reaching your goal and maintain a countdown to show the remaining time for people to contribute. People tend to leave things until the last minute and many generous donations come in just before the clock runs out when they feel they have the power to make or break your campaign.

9. A heartfelt finale:

Wrap up the campaign with a big thank you to everyone involved. Remember, fundraising is a collective effort, and appreciation goes a long way.

SUMMARY

The focused, sustained, and time-limited effort behind a campaign will boost any fundraising strategy, raising awareness and rallying support toward your cause. This chapter has shown you the power of campaigns for nonprofits and guided you through the most important steps to implement a successful campaign.

Think about your own campaigns. Are you currently planning one? Do you have one up and running? Analyze your current efforts through the lens of the information

I've provided you with and don't be afraid to change course if you see room for improvement.

In the next chapter, we'll shift gears and tackle the fifth fundraising strategy I want to share with you: annual giving.

8

STRATEGY #5: ANNUAL GIVING

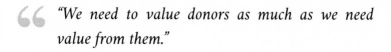 *"We need to value donors as much as we need value from them."*

— REINIER SPRUIT

When crafting your nonprofit's fundraising strategy, it's crucial to recognize the foundational role of annual giving. This ongoing and organized effort throughout the year allows donors to contribute multiple times, making it more than just a one-time gift. Unlike targeted campaigns or one-time donations, annual giving provides a reliable and consistent source of funding that supports day-to-day operations, sustains vital programs, and covers essential operating expenses.

Sometimes nonprofits overlook the significance of annual giving, focusing more on flashy campaigns. However, if you hope to keep things running, it's essential to acknowledge that annual giving is what keeps your organization running. It forms the backbone of your budget and ensures the sustainability of your programs and services.

In this chapter, I will show you the importance of annual giving and guide you in establishing a robust protocol that keeps the funds flowing consistently throughout the year. By understanding and prioritizing annual giving, you can build a solid foundation for your nonprofit's financial stability and long-term success.

WHY IS ANNUAL GIVING SO IMPORTANT FOR NONPROFITS?

1. Financial Stability:

Annual giving provides a reliable and steady source of income. By cultivating a broad base of regular donors, your organization will be able to generate consistent funding to support ongoing operations and programs. Stability is key if you hope to plan and budget effectively and is what makes work possible year after year. While grants or government funds may dry up, a strong network of reliable donors can keep an organization afloat and thriving even when things get hard.

2. Donor Engagement and Retention:

Regular contact and communication with supporters and donors are key to creating the sense of connection that makes annual giving possible. By keeping your donors updated on the impact of their contributions, you can strengthen loyalty and retain them over the long term.

3. Flexibility and Responsiveness:

Unlike funds raised through restricted campaigns, annual giving funds can be directed wherever they are most needed. Nonprofits can allocate these funds to cover operational expenses, invest in new initiatives, address emerging challenges, or fill gaps in underfunded areas. This flexibility enables organizations to adapt and respond to evolving needs and opportunities.

4. Mission Reinforcement:

Annual giving campaigns serve as powerful platforms to showcase and reinforce your nonprofit's mission and impact. The type of communication required by annual giving allows you to place the organization's core work in the spotlight.

5. Donor Benefits:

Annual giving offers tangible benefits for donors as well. Many countries provide tax deductions or incentives for charitable donations, making annual giving an attractive option for those seeking to maximize their philanthropic impact while reaping the potential financial benefits.

TYPES OF ANNUAL FUND PROGRAMS

Year-end fundraising, also known as the giving season, holds tremendous potential for nonprofits. In December alone, approximately one-third of annual giving occurs, and approximately 10% happens in a flurry during the last three days of the year (Donorbox, 2022). As people spend time giving gifts, spending time with family, and enjoying a renewed sense of community, they also feel inspired to give. Moreover, it's the final opportunity to make tax-deductible contributions for the calendar year. Plan well in advance to make the most of the year-end fundraising—even as early as in the previous quarter. Competition is fierce during this time, so you need to choose and disseminate compelling messaging. Make sure it's aligned with your broader mission, reinforcing your nonprofit's purpose and values. For example, a nonprofit focused on education may choose to highlight the transformative power of gifting educational resources to underprivileged children during the holiday season.

Sustainer programs are designed to cultivate long-term relationships with donors who commit to regular support, whether through monthly, quarterly, or other recurring contributions. With the convenience of automatic giving options like bank transfers, credit or debit cards, and workplace giving, becoming a sustainer has never been easier. These donors are among the most loyal supporters in your database and form the ideal bedrock for an annual fund. A sustainer program can take various approaches, such as converting one-time donors into recurring givers or encouraging existing donors to increase the frequency or amount of their contributions. Don't forget to provide incentives for increased participation. For example, a nonprofit focused on environmental conservation might provide access to behind-the-scenes footage or cute memes featuring the animals protected by the organization.

Viral fundraising initiatives harness the power of social media to create campaigns that spread rapidly and gain momentum. Since your nonprofit will appeal to donors throughout the year, keeping things fresh and engaging is key, finding new and innovative ways to capture their attention and inspire action. There's no guarantee that a campaign will go viral: sometimes the most well-thought-out campaigns can fall flat, while simple ones just ignite a spark. However, it's essential to remember that any piece of content has the potential to gain traction. Invest in quality communication materials, particularly videos, which can significantly amplify your annual giving efforts. For example, if your nonprofit is an animal rescue operation, you could create a heartwarming video showing the before and after of the animals you help save.

12 STEPS TO SUCCESSFULLY FUNDRAISE WITH ANNUAL INCENTIVES

Annual giving campaigns are just as pivotal a part of running a successful and sustainable nonprofit as capital and awareness campaigns are. After all, these programs are what make keeping the lights on possible. They pay for staff salaries, underfunded priorities, and daily expenses. So now that you're aware of their importance, let's dive into how to execute an engaging and successful annual giving initiative.

1. Set your goal:

All successful campaigns start with a clear target in mind and annual giving campaigns are no exception. Determine the amount you need and track your progress throughout the year. If this is your first annual giving venture, review last year's expenditure as a starting point. While you may not be aiming to cover all operating expenses, this will provide a benchmark to move forward.

2. Plan for success:

Once you have your annual goal set, break it down into smaller milestones. Consider dividing them by quarter or month. Timing is key: map out your annual fundraising efforts over the year, remembering how essential December is for fundraising. Be aware of any other campaigns by your nonprofit and draw a flexible plan that can be revised as the year progresses. Think beyond this year: a solid plan can be reused over and over again, saving time and energy.

3. Strategize and segment:

Determine the assets, resources, and channels you will need for your campaign. Will you be using traditional marketing avenues, digital outreach, or a mix of both? Consider developing targeted campaigns for specific segments like one-off donors, lapsed donors, young or elderly donors, and so on. You'll gain valuable data and insights into your donors' preferences. Keep in mind consistency: any segmented campaign should seamlessly integrate with the messaging in all others.

4. Research:

Analyze your current prospects so you can optimize your fundraising efforts. Identify and prioritize individuals who are most likely to have the resources and inclination to make significant contributions. Remember that major gifts can sometimes account for the majority of your funding. Don't forget about lapsed donors, as they could just need a nudge to re-engage. Personalize your communication and customize your asks accordingly. Keeping an updated database with as much information as possible is essential.

5. Recruit and organize your dream team:

Annual giving campaigns demand dedicated teams. Distribute responsibilities among them, focusing on the high-potential prospects you identified in the previous steps. Provide them with the tools they need to succeed.

Your annual giving initiative will likely encompass direct asks, marketing and outreach, and events. Consider recruiting volunteers and assign your experienced staffers as supervisors and coordinators. Don't forget to create a contingency plan to handle potential staff changes or leaves.

6. Craft compelling appeals:

It's now time to create impactful and compelling appeals that resonate with your prospects and donors. Utilize various channels, such as electronic or direct email, phone calls, and face-to-face conversations. Integrate your various marketing channels consistently but find creative ways to use each complementary so they don't feel repetitive. Harness the power of emotional story-telling to make your fundraiser come to life. Consider tying your appeals to key dates or occasions to add a sense of urgency. Maintain regular communication throughout the year, but up your game in December: it's a busy and competitive month but can yield great results.

7. Nurture major donor relationships:

Face-to-face requests often occur at the end of culti-vating major donors. Approach these requests with care. A face-to-face ask should never come as a surprise. It should be the natural next step, an extension of previous communications and touch points. Nurture these special relationships: engage your existing donors, considering their giving history, personal background, and indicators of wealth. Tailor your engagement accordingly.

8. Monitor and optimize:

Regularly check your campaign metrics to track progress toward your overall goal. Assess the performance of individual campaign items, like specific advertisements, newsletters, videos, etc. Don't be afraid to tinker with something that's not working or dropping an unsuccessful strategy that's consuming energy and resources. Optimize your strategy based on data and testing. While it's beneficial to improve upon a base blueprint each year, inject excitement by introducing surprises. Keep your campaign fresh, interesting, and engaging.

9. Optimize the donation process:

Donating should be a seamless and fast experience. Your online donation platform should be user-friendly and optimized with sharing buttons. Not everyone will know how much to give. Provide preset donation levels while allowing for custom donations. Highlight the impact of each level and emphasize the importance of annual giving.

10. Engage your donors:

Inform donors about the impact of their contribution: this is particularly important for first-time donors. If the donation is substantial, a call or handwritten note is a good idea. Seek their input and feedback to make them feel valued. Follow up in the upcoming weeks or months, emphasizing key dates such as the anniversary of their gift. This will build rapport and trust—the key to nurturing long-term giving relationships.

11. Promote recurring giving:

Retaining donors is easier than attracting new ones. Encourage recurring giving options with strategies such as a simple tick box on a form, a PS in a written communication, an actionable button in your newsletter, or a follow-up ask. Consider offering perks or benefits to regular supporters, who make up the core of your donor base. It could be a membership program with various tiers based on giving level or longevity. Brainstorm ways to show recognition, fostering a sense of belonging which will translate into a habit of giving. Access to exclusive content, merchandise, or special events is always appealing. Capture pledges from donors who commit to future contributions, creating guidelines to secure additional funds. These may be unconditional or contingent on the nonprofit meeting certain conditions.

12. Explore business support:

Don't overlook the potential of corporate support. Start with low-hanging fruit—businesses with an existing connection to your nonprofit. Make use of any connections your staff or board members may have and recruit your top supporters to help you make new contacts. Seek companies that are aligned to your mission and core values and tap into their corporate social responsibility budgets. Understand their budget cycles, priorities, and expectations for charitable partnerships. Refer to the partnerships chapter for a refresher.

SUMMARY

Annual giving is the backbone of your fundraising efforts, providing you a chance to showcase your mission. Tackle these campaigns through the various channels available, such as events, meetings, phone calls, direct mail, and digital media. While annual giving campaigns require significant time and resources, the payoff is worth it: increased awareness and visibility of your cause, donor acquisition, enhanced donor participation, and invaluable insights into what inspires and resonates with the public. As you've learned, strike the delicate balance between integrating and segmenting your multiple channels and campaigns.

This chapter has taught you about the importance of developing a strategic, long-term approach to day-to-day operations, keeping options open for your nonprofit throughout the year.

Think about your own annual giving fundraising efforts: Are you keeping your database updated? Do you have devoted team members? Do you have a yearly plan that's easy to update? Revise your own processes and improve them following the guidelines I've provided. Let's now shift gears and explore the key elements for hosting a successful fundraising event.

I hope that you're finding *Nonprofit Fundraising Strategies* useful. If you have feedback, whether positive or negative, please leave a review. My goal is to provide the best possible books for you, and your reviews are crucial in achieving that.

9

STRATEGY #6: EVENT HOSTING

When people think of fundraising for nonprofits, events are often what immediately comes to mind. While they are often seen as the highlight of fundraising, the reality is that planning and executing a successful event requires a tremendous amount of effort. And the reality is that even with substantial budgeting planning, even experienced event planners can struggle to achieve a reasonable profit.

There's just no way around it: hosting events is not for the faint of heart. However, with proper organization, they can be simpler to pull off than you might expect—as well as being very rewarding, both financially and to your organization. Whether dinners, galas, auctions, tournaments, car washes, concerts, cook-offs, or carnivals, successful events can become so renowned that they overshadow the organizations themselves, like the case of March of Dimes, which changed its name to align with its prominent fundraising event. Events bring people together, attracting new donors and partners, and rekindling existing support. The group setting reduces the pressure typically associated with face-to-face solicitations while maintaining a personal connection by putting names to faces in real life. Moreover, they are enjoyable and exciting to existing members, fostering a sense of belonging and community. When combined with a well-executed PR strategy, an event can significantly enhance an organization's profile. Event organizers can align events with their fundraising calendar, facilitating staff and volunteer engagement, collaboration, and celebration at the conclusion of a campaign. If your organization deals with urgent needs, such as emergency responses to natural disasters, events can be the natural way to go.

This chapter will provide you with a straightforward strategy to organize successful events, which you can easily tailor to your unique circumstances. With these guidelines, you will be well equipped to host your next event, raising awareness, garnering community support, and securing funding for your mission.

TYPES OF FUNDRAISING EVENTS

Fundraising events can be categorized into two main types:

1. Events that are specific to your organization and target individuals already invested in your cause. These events clearly communicate attendees will be asked to make donations and often have a fixed amount.

2. Community-oriented events, where fundraising is incorporated at the start, with participants paying to participate. Think of bake sales or sporting events, which will leave attendees with a positive experience and predispose them to spread the word. If your organization is on the smaller size, fun runs or walks are easy to plan and organize, while concerts and live events are better suited for organizations with larger budgets (Finch, 2015).

Short of ideas on what to organize? Here are some of my favorites, along with some caveats to consider before embarking on one :

Galas are large-scale fundraisers often hosted by nonprofits once a year as a signature event. They typically include dinner, entertainment, and a raffle or auction. Planning a gala requires substantial time and upfront investment, including scouting facilities, arranging MCs, planning menus, and organizing presentations. Funds are raised through ticket sales, either individual tickets or entire tables, and sometimes through sponsorships. Since they can be expensive, they tend to be the domain of larger nonprofits. Things like catering costs, staff requirements, rental and venue fees, as well as the costs of promoting and marketing the event can quickly add up. However, the average return is also generally higher when compared to other types of events.

As I mentioned, while **auctions** can be part of a gala event, they can also be standalone fundraising events. In an auction, items are sold to the highest bidder, and nonprofits often solicit donated goods from businesses to auction off. Depending on the scale, a lot may go into planning an auction, or it may be relatively low effort. You can organize an online-only auction through a platform that handles bids, notifies winners, and manages logistics on your behalf—however, be aware that they will generally take a cut.

A twist on the traditional auction is the **silent auction**. Goods are displayed for inspection, and attendees write down their bids. Mystery boxes or bags are a clever way to add intrigue and excitement to the auction by combining smaller items.

Marathons are popular and versatile fundraising events for your community. They don't have to be strenuous: walk-a-thons, dance-a-thons, golf-a-thons, or bike-a-thons are usually fun, family affairs. They also have the lowest cost per dollar raised ratio (Finch, 2015), delivering the most bang for your buck. Planning a marathon event requires minimal effort, making them the perfect type of fundraising event for smaller teams and nonprofits. Participants raise funds by seeking sponsorships from their personal and professional networks, often fostering friendly competition. Donations can come from anywhere in the world, not just from the event's location. Your nonprofit will often be responsible for organizing prizes and sponsors, managing sign-ups, providing encouragement, tracking results, and potentially hosting a celebration after the event.

Online fundraising events are a great complement and can even replace in-person events. These include crowdfunding challenges, virtual game nights, concerts, workshops, or trivia nights. Organizing an online event is typically less resource-intensive compared to live events, as you can utilize technology that your nonprofit already uses. Online events also tend to be more inclusive and accessible, as you can include features like closed captions, transcripts, and screen reader accommodations, which might be particularly important—depending on the work of your organization. Virtual a-thon events allow participants worldwide to take part at their convenience and can span several days or even weeks—unlike in-person events. Add an element of competition to increase the participants' commitment to the campaign. The ultimate goal is to collect donations through your website, ensuring a smooth and seamless process.

Art exhibits can be relatively easy to plan, although they are better suited for mid-sized or larger nonprofits. A charitable art show can take the form of a competition where artists pay an entry fee to showcase their work for judging. Prizes for the winners can be donated by local businesses. Alternatively, you can recruit artists to display their work for sale, with a percentage of sales being donated to your nonprofit. Inviting well-known artists can attract more interest and maximize the potential success of your art exhibit fundraiser.

Sporting events also serve as effective fundraisers for nonprofits. You could simply set up a concession stall at a local football, basketball, or baseball game, and offer snacks and drinks, taking home a percentage of the sales. The atmosphere at a stadium is typically spirited and communal, which can foster donations. However, while these events can be fun, the return on investment may not be as strong. Another option is to organize a tournament or host a fun run/walk. Consider partnering with a local team to auction off their time, allowing people to bid for individuals or the entire team. Local athletes could also donate their time for various activities, from chores to running a fitness class. All proceeds go toward your nonprofit under this scheme.

Lastly, **donor appreciation events** are held to express gratitude, highlight the impact of donor support, and strengthen donor relationships. These events are free for attending donors, focusing on building rapport and suggesting other ways advocates can contribute without a direct ask for monetary donations.

13 STEPS TO HOSTING A SUCCESSFUL EVENT

Hosting a successful fundraising event requires careful planning and execution. Mid to large nonprofits have an advantage when it comes to hosting events, thanks to their bigger budgets and diverse teams. Nevertheless, and even if your organization is small and/or new to the world of event planning, following these key steps will help you achieve a strong return on investment and make it a success:

1. Form a planning and hosting committee:

Establish a main team responsible for executing the event and create subcommittees that will handle different aspects of the fundraiser, such as production, promotion, and fundraising. Collaborate closely to ensure seamless coordination and execution. Establish a planning committee, charged with behind-the-scenes tasks, and a host committee, which will focus on fundraising and donor recruitment. You should also have an event day committee that's responsible for the big day itself.

2. Define the purpose and goals:

Determine the main purpose of your fundraiser, whether it's increasing visibility, raising funds, or thanking supporters. Choose an event type, date, and budget that aligns with your goals. Consider the audience, mission, fundraising targets, available resources, and expertise when deciding on the event type. This can help you decide what will make for a compelling event and your metrics for success.

3. Build an event budget and timeline:

Develop a rough outline of the event budget and create a project timeline. These will evolve over time, but having a preliminary plan will provide a foundation for organizing the event.

4. Research costs and suppliers:

Identify the requirements for your event and research potential costs and suppliers. This includes securing a venue, setting a theme, arranging for decor, consumables, entertainment, photographers, and other necessary elements. Consider your target audience and their interests, as well as your fundraising goal and budget. It's great to shoot for the stars, but don't run before you can walk—work your way up to that annual gala.

5. Recruit sponsors and partners:

Reach out to potential sponsors and partners to support your event. Tailor your outreach to each organization, highlighting the benefits they will receive from supporting your cause. Any additional funding or gifts you are able to line up at this stage will ensure your budget stretches as far as possible. For example, if you are planning a charity run, you could ask a sporting goods store to sponsor the event and potentially provide some athletic gear for prizes.

6. Plan, plan, plan:

Plan and organize your event to the very last details. The list is long and includes securing a location and setting a theme, then tackling décor, consumables, entertainment, and photographers, among others. Remember that high-profile performers or professionals may have a busy schedule, so contact them early. Check with local regulation and food compliance norms. Virtual events usually don't have so many items, but you will still need to plan. Adapt engagement techniques for virtual platforms, such as icebreakers, polls, quizzes, and breakout chat rooms. Break down all considerations into categories to ensure nothing is overlooked.

7. Get people talking:

It's now time to promote the event. Design and deploy promotional materials both physical and digital, including posters, flyers, social media graphics, emails, web pages, and forms. As you start promoting the event through your marketing channels, you can also reach out to local media to expand your target audience and encourage partners, sponsors, staff, volunteers, and advocates to spread the word.

8. Organize volunteers:

Recruit volunteers to help with the event. From selling tickets or enlisting participants through to cleaning up after the event itself, enthusiastic volunteers are essential.

Assign roles for ticket sales, participant management, event setup, attendee assistance, and post-event cleanup.

9. Conduct a dress rehearsal:

Schedule a dry run to practice ahead of time to ensure everything is running smoothly between staff, volunteers, vendors, and anyone else involved. Create a detailed playbook for the event, listing each step and responsible individuals.

10. Use the event as an engagement opportunity:

Emphasize your nonprofit's mission and provide opportunities for attendees to understand how they can help beyond the immediate fundraising goal. This is a great time to request annual pledges and consolidate long-term commitments. Provide progress reports throughout the event and try to gather additional support to reach your goal.

11. Follow up and say thanks:

The work doesn't end when everyone leaves. As I've said over and over throughout this book, promoting long-term relationships with your donors is essential. Share post-event updates on social media, thanking participants and donors. Send personalized thank you letters acknowledging their attendance and generosity. Don't forget to ask for feedback: donors like to feel like they have a say in the future of the nonprofit. Cultivate a long-term connection with attendees: almost a third of offline-only, first-time donors are retained for more than a year, which is slightly higher than 25% of online-only new donors (Double the Donation, 2022).

12. Evaluate and debrief:

Take stock of the event afterward—calculate the total funds raised, expenses, attendance, and net profit. Depending on the size of your organization and events, you might choose to organize the information in a basic spreadsheet or pay for specific software designed for fundraising and event management. This investment will make things easier in the future. Run a debrief with your committees to review the event's success and areas for improvement.

13. Acknowledge event contributors:

Recognize and appreciate everyone involved and make sure to pay any outstanding debts with providers. Give special thanks to the event coordinator, who would have held the most stressful position of all, for their significant role and dedication.

SUMMARY

Events are one of the best ways to foster connection, raise substantial funds, and build a community with your donors and supporters. They are a high-effort but a potentially high-return way to raise awareness and money, and many nonprofits have developed a reputation for hosting impactful, profitable, long-running events.

In this chapter, you've learned about the various types of fundraising events and how to organize a successful one. Remember to capitalize on the momentum your fundraising event creates. Continue to engage with new and renewed contacts and nurture your relationship with them over time.

Think about the events you've organized in the past and recognize room for improvement where possible. Assess your capabilities and strengths as a nonprofit and organize the right type of event for you. As I have explained, bigger is not always better. Begin by testing the water and move toward larger and more demanding events.

In the next chapter, I will explore the final fundraising strategy in this book. We will focus on the significance of donor retention and the strategies involved in cultivating sustainable long-term giving relationships. Donor retention is a crucial aspect of fundraising, as maintaining existing donors tends to be more cost-effective and efficient compared to acquiring new ones. By building strong relationships with donors and fostering their continued support, organizations can ensure ongoing financial stability and make a greater impact on their missions.

10

STRATEGY #7: DONOR RETENTION AND MANAGEMENT

> *"The manner of giving is worth more than the gift."*
>
> — PIERRE CORNEILLE

Just as customers are the lifeblood of a business, donors are what keep a nonprofit afloat. For any charitable organization, loyal and consistent supporters who donate regularly are invaluable. But these kinds of relationships don't just spring up out of nowhere. Cultivating such relationships requires effort and dedication from you and your staff. Building trust and nurturing the seeds of a mutually beneficial long-term relationship is an ongoing process that is essential to the survival of any nonprofit.

Strong donor retention is essential for an organization's financial health and stability. It enables your nonprofit to plan more effectively by providing predictable income, which facilitates accurate forecasting and budgeting from year to year. A higher donor retention rate also means a larger donor database to work with and more prospects for planning major campaigns or soliciting significant contributions.

In this chapter, I will delve into the importance of donor retention and share with you some key steps to ensure you will keep your donors happy. If you've ever struggled with planning and budgeting or have felt the burnout of constantly having to acquire new donors, then this is the right chapter for you.

WHAT IS DONOR RETENTION AND WHY DOES IT MATTER?

We'll define donor retention as the number or percentage of donors who continue giving to your nonprofit, as opposed to those who stop after their initial gift. You can calculate your donor retention rate by dividing the number of repeat donors this year by the number of people who donated last year. For example, if you have 220 donors in a single year and only 79 out of those give again in the following period, then your donor retention rate would be 36%.

A higher retention rate means maintaining a consistent supporter base year after year, reducing the pressure to continually acquire new donors. This is key because, in reality, many organizations either lose money or barely break even on the first donation from a new donor.

The value of a newly acquired donor lies not only in the immediate gift but also in unlocking long-term giving potential. If you manage to secure a second donation, often referred to as the golden donation, the likelihood of retaining that donor on an ongoing basis significantly improves. Not only does it cost less to keep a donor than to find a new one, but previous donors are also more likely to give more. Their initial donation is rarely their largest, and as their affinity toward your cause deepens, they are more likely to contribute in significant ways. Major gifts, in particular, are the result of a lasting long-term relationship. Long-term donors may also volunteer at events, join your board, or spread the word about your mission without prompting.

So what's a good retention rate? Nonprofits have an average donor retention rate of about 45%, although it's worth noting that retention rates for new donors are even lower, around 30% (Bloomerang, 2022). No organization is entirely immune to attrition or losing donors. It is unrealistic to expect a 100% retention rate. That's why it is so crucial to balance donor acquisition efforts with donor retention initiatives.

Ignoring donor retention may not seem like a problem in the short term, but it is a mistake that will hurt in the long run. As your donor pool shrinks over time, so do the dollars. Even a seemingly small fluctuation in your donor retention rate can represent significant losses in donations. And, unfortunately, once someone stops giving, the chances of them returning are slim.

DONOR STEWARDSHIP

Donor stewardship refers to the process of developing and nurturing a relationship with a donor after their initial gift. Stewardship means to supervise or take care of and that is exactly what your nonprofit is doing: stewarding each donor, with the ultimate goal of encouraging them to give again. Donor stewardship also involves attending to simple yet essential tasks, like properly stewarding a donor's personal information—keeping their details secure, processing their gifts correctly, and directing those funds toward the purpose the donor expected the money to go toward.

Donors want to feel appreciated and know that their contributions make a difference. But they are more than their gifts; they are also potential advocates for your mission. Your role is to create a compelling donor experience that makes them feel like an integral part of a special mission or community, encouraging them to give repeatedly and stay connected to your nonprofit. The worst-case scenario is when donors fall into the "out-of-sight, out-of-mind" category. Donors often lapse because of factors like lack of acknowledgment or lack of ongoing communication—two very preventable mistakes.

It is crucial to have a clear process in place not only for what happens immediately after someone donates but also for the subsequent information that is sent to them and when it is sent. A donor stewardship program should include recognition, relationship building, managing gifts according to donor intentions, and reporting back on the impact of their contribution. As you can see and as with all relationships in life, it all comes back to communication.

Keep your donors informed about your organization's work, outcomes, and how they can continue to engage and contribute. Acknowledge the impact their support has on your charity's mission and offer various avenues for involvement beyond monetary contributions. Remember that someone's capacity to give may fluctuate over time as their life circumstances change.

While it is great to move a donor up the value ladder—that is, increasing the size of their gifts—not everyone is in a position to give more. There are numerous ways, beyond financial support, through which individuals can contribute to a cause. Ensure your donors are aware of these options and invite them to get involved beyond their wallets and credit cards. People are donating to your organization because they believe in the cause you support: provide them with opportunities to be more involved. Embrace these ebbs and flows, as donor stewardship is not a strictly linear process.

It should go without saying, but not all of your communications should involve requests for donations. Make it clear that you care about more than just financial contributions. Create various communication channels and leverage them to establish multiple touch points, whether through direct mail, digital platforms, text messages, or phone calls. Engaging donors through these channels helps them feel connected, seen, and heard—essential steps in cultivating loyal supporters.

Lastly, I want to emphasize that donor stewardship is not a process that should be confined to isolated silos but integrated into your nonprofit's broader communication strategy. For example, if a donor has just received a thank you message, rather than immediately sending them information about your latest fundraising campaign, it may be more appropriate to wait or inform them about a different aspect, such as your upcoming major event. If your nonprofit has different departments or a number of people in charge of sending out communications, you must ensure a delicate balance and coordination so that all messages are well-timed and strategic.

Implementing effective donor stewardship may seem daunting, particularly for smaller organizations. However, small nonprofits must prioritize donor retention as well. In fact, stewarding a smaller donor base is often more manageable than managing a larger one. If you are new to stewardship, read on for a straightforward plan you can start to roll out right away.

11 STEPS TO MAINTAINING DONOR RETENTION

Developing and implementing a structured approach to donor retention is essential for your nonprofit to maintain consistency in your efforts, even when team members change over time. These are proven steps to establish a successful and enduring donor retention program:

1. Assign a dedicated team:

Expecting staff to fit these tasks in whenever they can means they will likely fall between the cracks. Designate specific individuals or at least one person in a smaller nonprofit to focus on donor relations. Additionally, consider investing in donor management software to streamline retention initiatives and ensure accurate data management. Technology can automate simple, repetitive tasks, ensure accuracy, and reduce human error, ultimately helping your team focus on and achieve your goals.

2. Evaluate your retention rate:

Assess how long your existing donors typically continue to support your organization. Lapsing donors are like funding leaks, impacting your organization's financial stability. By improving retention, you will enhance your nonprofit's bottom line. And without tracking it, you won't improve.

3. Plan your retention program:

Define your strategy for engaging donors. Outline the frequency, type, and channels of communication that will create an ideal donor experience. Research (Bloomerang, 2022) suggests that making phone contact within 90 days improves retention rates and the likelihood of receiving a second donation, often referred to as the "golden donation." Ask your trusted donors and supporters how they feel about your follow-up communication and look for areas for improvement.

4. Personalize donor outreach:

Segment your donor database into key groups such as major donors, long-time donors, lapsed donors, and new donors. Tailor your communications to each segment based on their preferences and interests. Begin the conversation by asking about their well-being and take the time to get to know them. Find out how they heard about your organization, why they were drawn to it, and why they chose to give. Record this information, so you can revisit the topics you discussed in conversation.

5. Say thanks:

Express gratitude for their support, acknowledge their contributions, and connect their donations to your nonprofit's larger mission. Highlight upcoming events, campaigns, and opportunities for involvement, and extend an invitation to stay engaged.

6. Create a welcome kit:

Develop a digital or physical welcome kit to nurture the donor relationship. While a physical one can feel more personal and can help them express their support offline as well, an electronic version will be easier to automate. Welcome them to your family of supporters; make them feel part of a thriving community. Your welcome kit can include past newsletters, educational material about your cause, and resources that can help them become effective advocates. Design shareable social media graphics to make it easy for donors to spread the word about your organization. Invite them to participate in your upcoming initiatives and share your calendar to date.

7. Maintain high-value communications:

Regularly send personalized communications to maintain strong donor relations. Let donors witness the impact of their gifts by framing their contributions as crucial to achieving your nonprofit's mission. Provide updates on your nonprofit's work, volunteer opportunities, events, and reports to deepen the relationship. Emphasize the specific outcomes and express gratitude on their behalf. If you have reached a milestone as an organization, share it with your donors. For instance, rather than stating *"We provided food and vaccinations for 10 rescue dogs thanks to your donation,"* phrase it as *"Your generous gift provided food and vaccinations for these 10 rescue dogs. On their behalf, thank you for your support."* The more specific, the better.

8. Respect their time:

Balance keeping them informed while respecting their time and privacy by allowing donors to select their communication preferences. Lots of people unsubscribe from newsletters because they feel overwhelmed: don't overdo it. If you see supporters and donors unsubscribing from your communications, it's time to reassess content and strategy. Allow them to choose how often they would like to hear from you, so they feel they're in control of communications.

9. Show genuine care and appreciation:

Demonstrate that your organization values donors as individuals by providing tokens of gratitude. Feature donors on your website, dedicate social media posts to highlight their generosity, or create videos showcasing the impact of their donations. Celebrate milestones such as birthdays or anniversaries with personalized cards or notes. Make the time to personally reach out to high-value, recurring donors with a handwritten note or phone call.

10. Foster a sense of community:

Organize events specifically dedicated to recognizing and appreciating donors. Use these events to connect with donors personally, learn more about their interests and motivations, and express gratitude face-to-face. These events also foster a sense of community among donors, allowing them to connect with one another. Use the opportunity to share a high-impact video or speech about your work and the impact of their donations. Some organizations find that running some type of membership, society, or club is also an effective way to create a community. Typically, members give time or money in exchange for certain insider benefits such as early access to information, merchandise, or exclusive events.

11. Measure and adapt:

Continually evaluate the success of your retention program and make necessary adjustments. Monitor metrics such as email open rates and the percentage of donors who volunteer. Use the data to inform decision-making and improve key performance indicators. Aim for consistent retention rates while striving for improvement.

SUMMARY

Donor retention is an important indicator of financial health and stability. Bringing in new donors takes a lot of effort, time, and resources, so don't waste them. As I've emphasized before, investing in keeping donors happy and emotionally involved will pay off financially. While it may seem like a lot of work, the rewards are worth it.

To ensure your success, it is imperative to focus on developing a robust donor stewardship program. Take a moment to evaluate your current approach: are you methodically examining this process step by step, or are you simply improvising? Review the steps I have provided and assign specific responsibilities within your organization. Regular and strategic communication plays a pivotal role in establishing connections, fostering trust, and cultivating loyalty—the foundation of a mutually satisfying donor relationship. Your ultimate objective should be to engage each donor meaningfully and personally. In the next chapter, we will address the most common questions related to nonprofit fundraising.

11. THE FUNDRAISING FAQ

> "Giving is not just about making a donation, it's about making a difference."
>
> — KATHY CALVIN

If you have read this far, fully immersing yourself in the preceding chapters, you will have developed a solid understanding of the seven fundraising strategies I recommend. You will have a clear view of the nuances of the donor-charity relationship and how to consistently nurture givers through a variety of means. Let's round off by answering some of the top questions commonly asked when it comes to the mechanisms of nonprofit fundraising.

HOW DO YOU ASK FOR DONATIONS?

There are many ways you can ask prospective donors to give to your cause. In this book, we've covered seven major strategies that organizations of any size and type can use to their benefit. Nonprofits utilize many campaign tactics, like membership drives, pledging programs, mail appeals, major gift campaigns, canvassing, phone appeals, etc. They may also seek grants or contributions (including payroll giving or gift matching) from corporates, foundations, government, or other agencies: businesses, religious, civic, or community groups.

Your belief in your cause must overcome the discomfort of asking someone for money. Remember who you are truly raising funds for —the beneficiaries of your work and the communities you serve. Make the case larger than your nonprofit. Highlight how individuals and communities will be positively impacted—whether through new educational opportunities, economic development, community pride, or improved quality of life. Show how a donation is an investment in a brighter future.

ARE THERE CERTAIN RULES ON HOW MUCH FUNDRAISING A NONPROFIT CAN DO?

In fact, public charities must derive at least a third of their support from the public. In other words, your organization cannot rely too much on contributions that come from people closely involved with it, such as founders, board members, or employees. This is another reason why it is important to prioritize fundraising. It is also beneficial to diversify your revenue base. Receiving income from a wide range of donors and partners is a good thing for your organization's financial health.

HOW DOES A NONPROFIT GET REGISTERED TO FUNDRAISE?

There are certain requirements of nonprofits when it comes to raising funds from the general public. These requirements and regulations are meant to provide transparency for donors, providing protection from potential fraud or misrepresentation. They also allow nonprofits to minimize their tax obligations.

Not all states require registration before you begin to raise funds there. Some types of nonprofits are exempt from state registration, such as certain educational, religious, or membership organizations; revenue criteria may also be applicable. And if you have recently created a nonprofit organization and are still awaiting your 501(c)(3) status, this will not necessarily prohibit you from beginning fundraising activities; however, contributions will not be tax-deductible until your nonprofit is officially recognized as a charity. That said, it may be preferable to wait until your official registration status is confirmed. It is always wise to check the requirements as they pertain to your circumstances and conduct research and planning in advance before getting started.

To register your nonprofit, start by doing so in the state where you are based. You will need to submit a registration statement and supporting documentation to each state agency. You will typically be asked for basic information about your nonprofit and its finances, and potentially, officers or directors; most of this will then be available to the public. You can then proceed to register in any other states where you have a physical presence or where you might solicit donations.

WHAT DO WE NEED TO KNOW ABOUT RAISING FUNDS BEYOND STATE LINES?

When raising funds across state boundaries, you must adhere to the rules in each state. Register your organization in every state where you will be asking for donations. This applies to online fundraisers, not just in-person fundraising. Running a national or digital campaign will require you to register in every single state. Some states accept the Unified Registration Statement, but given the varying requirements, deadlines, and fees across states, this may or may not save you time.

WHAT CAN WE DO TO ENSURE THE SUCCESS OF OUR FUNDRAISING CAMPAIGN?

In times gone by, many nonprofits relied on methods like telethons, phone appeals, direct mail, and collecting donations at events. Now, there are many more ways to get people involved. You can and should strategically solicit donations in many ways, especially now that the internet has opened up the entire world.

Start planning ahead, promoting your campaign early, and spreading the word. The more people who hear about it, the more success you are likely to have. Make full use of your database, of your existing supporters and stakeholders, and even local press and businesses. Getting coverage in the form of a news story can go a long way, as can posters or flyers displayed in high-traffic areas. Optimize your website, landing pages, and donation forms to capture interest and donations. Don't be afraid of oversaturating your social media or experi-

172 | JAMES RUELL

menting with advertising. Remember that people generally need to be exposed to a message multiple times before they are inclined to act on it.

Adapt your approach, tone, and messaging as needed based on the channel and audience. What you say on a flyer will differ from how you communicate in a short online video, or how you speak to a representative at a business or foundation about gaining their financial support. While we may think of fundraising as asking a stranger for money, this is not the ideal way to approach it. Where possible, it is preferable to cultivate a relationship before making the request (and certainly to continue to nurture it afterward).

HOW DO WE ENSURE THAT OUR CAMPAIGNING IS COMPLETELY LEGAL?

Every country's laws will differ, but a variety of resources offer in-depth guidelines on navigating fundraising laws as a nonprofit. For instance, refer to the US Council of Nonprofits, Gov.UK, or Australia's Funding Centre.

Here are a few general pointers to keep in mind. For in-person fundraisers, you must procure the appropriate license for any event you are holding. A permit is usually needed to hold a fundraising event in a public place, and the minimum age for street collectors is usually 16. If taking place on private property, which includes shopping centers, you need permission beforehand from the owner or manager. This also applies to collection boxes. A license is required to serve alcohol and may be needed for a game of chance, such as a raffle or auction.

For online fundraisers, you will need to comply with privacy and anti-spam laws, such as the CAN-SPAM Act. Ensure people have truly opted in before you email them and make it clear how they can unsubscribe. The state of California (California Consumer Privacy Act) and the European Union (General Data Protection Regulations) outline additional regulations you may need to account for and keep in mind. Always err on the side of caution to ensure compliance.

WHAT INFORMATION MUST WE INCLUDE IN OUR FUNDRAISING MATERIALS?

It is important to ensure your fundraising materials include any and all legally required information, such as your registered charity status or number, full name, and registered office address. In many states, you must tell prospective donors how they can obtain a copy of your nonprofit's official financial filings. In addition to the disclosures you are required to display, think more

174 | JAMES RUELL

broadly about the impression your fundraising collateral will make on a donor.

There you have it: a comprehensive guide to strategies for successful fundraising. Use this as a reference you can return to at any point to refresh your memory or to find new ideas.

CONCLUSION

Nonprofits play an essential role in today's world. They provide vital resources and programs for people and causes that may not be served otherwise because they are not commercially profitable. In other words, nonprofits operate for the public good, and their work ensures healthier, stronger, and more vibrant communities for the future.

No matter what field you operate in, the size of your organization, or the length of your tenure—fundraising must be a top priority for your nonprofit, year after year. It is imperative to maintain focus on acquiring and retaining donors, continuing the tactics that have brought success, and experimenting with new ones to fuel further growth. When fundraising is at the forefront of your strategy, you are investing in the long-term health and sustainability of your organization. Financial stability is what will ensure your team can continue doing this work and making an impact.

Fundraising is not a mysterious black box endeavor. It simply boils down to understanding and connecting with donors, inspiring them to give, and investing in the ongoing relationship so they continue to stay connected and contribute. I have outlined seven key strategies here: partnerships, bringing in donors, online fundraisers, campaigns, annual giving, event hosting, and donor retention and stewardship. You will have noticed that the key principles underlying all these are similar, as these are universal.

Every strategy begins with deliberate planning. Get clear on your goal. How much do you want to raise? What are you fundraising for? Why would someone want to give? Set specific, measurable, realistic objectives. Aim high, but don't overreach. Success breeds success, and with each win, you can expand your horizon further.

Lead by centering your audience, always keeping them at the forefront of any initiative. Understanding who they are and what they are interested in should inform everything about how you interact with them. This applies not just to your core campaign message, but also to the channels or platforms you use to communicate with them. Go where they are, rather than trying to get them to come to you. The more you do this, the higher the likelier reward.

Once you decide on what type of fundraiser to host, you will need to dive into the next level of detail. How much will this cost? What is the timeline? What resources are needed to execute? Make use of nonprofit technology to streamline workflow and automate tasks and try your hand at some of the popular fundraising platforms available today—like Fundly, Donately, Qgiv, and others listed earlier.

Follow up with donors to express thanks. Always be upfront about where the funds are going. Whether someone gives $10 or $1,000, they desire and deserve to know how it will be used. So, whether their donation will fund a new animal shelter, books for underprivileged youth, or clean drinking water for families, get specific and give them a tangible image to connect to. Set the tone for your ongoing communication upfront, and then follow through with regular updates that help build trust, credibility, and the relationship.

Conduct a debrief after the fundraiser concludes to analyze the results. This allows for both celebration of successes and identifying opportunities to improve. Finally, I encourage you to treasure your team, both staff and volunteers. They are the engine of your fundraising efforts. And great leaders who have the heart and drive to raise substantial funds are a rare breed. Never take their effort for granted.

Now that you understand what fundraising is truly about and the tools it takes to successfully solicit donations for your nonprofit, you too have what it takes to execute the next Ice Bucket Challenge or March of Dimes. As you reach the end of this book, please consider writing a review online and sharing your honest opinion. If it has helped you in some way, then many more organizations out there could also benefit from hearing about it. Fundraising is a foundational pillar for any nonprofit; mastering this skill and incorporating the strategies outlined in this book will enable you to bring your mission to life at a larger scale. Keep this book as a guide —a blueprint as you continue on your fundraising journey—as the tools and strategies shared here are time-less principles you can continue to leverage regardless of the economic environment, year after year.

NOTES

5. STRATEGY #2: BRINGING IN DONORS

1. For a thorough immersion into the world of grants and a playbook for how to improve your application success rate, refer to my other book, *Winning Grants: How to Write Winning Grant Proposals That Will Get You Funding for Your Nonprofit.*

OTHER BOOKS BY JAMES RUELL

(AVAILABLE ON AMAZON & AUDIBLE)

WINNING

GRANTS

How to Write Winning Grant Proposals
That Will Get You Funding for
Your Nonprofit

JAMES RUELL

Winning Grants: How to Write Winning Grant Proposals That Will Get You Funding for Your Nonprofit

The 12 Secrets of

Exceptional
Nonprofit
Leaders

**The Key Traits Necessary to Drive Social
Impact**

James Ruell

*The 12 Secrets of Exceptional Nonprofit Leaders: The Key Traits
Necessary to Drive Social Impact*

REFERENCES

ALS. (2021). ALS Ice Bucket Challenge Commitments. https://www.als.org/ice-bucket-challenge-spending.

America's Charities. Facts & Statistics on Workplace Giving, Matching Gifts, and Volunteer Programs.

Bloomerang. (2022). Actually, Calling Donors To Thank Them Does Make Them More Likely To Give Again (And Give More). https://bloomerang.co/blog/actually-calling-donors-to-thank-them-does-make-them-more-likely-to-give-again-and-give-more/.

Bloomerang. (2022). A Guide to Donor Retention. https://bloomerang.co/blog/donor-retention/.

Candid. (2020). Key Facts on U.S. Nonprofits and Foundations. https://www.issuelab.org/resources/36381/36381.pdf

Double The Donation. (2022). Corporate Giving and Matching Gift Statistics. https://doublethedonation.com/matching-gift-statistics.

Donorbox. (2022). 13 Steps to The Perfect Year-End Giving Campaign in 2022. https://donorbox.org/nonprofit-blog/year-end-giving .

Ebarb, T. (2019). Nonprofits Fail – Here's Seven Reasons Why. National Association of Nonprofit Organizations & Executives (NANOE). https://nanoe.org/nonprofits-fail/.

Ewing Marion Kauffman Foundation. (2017). Nonprofit Effectiveness Initiative Research: Online Survey of Nonprofit Organizations – Report of Findings. https://www.kauffman.org/wp-content/uploads/2019/09/2017_Kauffman_Nonprofit_Effectiveness_Survey_Report_pdf.pdf .

Finch, J. (2015). Fundraising Management Software User Report. Software Advice. https://www.softwareadvice.com/nonprofit/userview/fundraising-management-report-2015.

Finch, J. (2015). Which Fundraising Event Is Best for Your Nonprofit? Software Advice. https://www.softwareadvice.com/nonprofit/industryview/fundraising-event-report-2015/.

Georgia Tech. (2014). Face It: Instagram Pictures With Faces are More Popular. https://news.gatech.edu/news/2014/03/20/face-it-instagram-pictures-faces-are-more-popular.

Network for Good. (2018). 7 Reasons Why Donors Give (and 1 Reason They Don't). https://www.networkforgood.com/resource/7-reasons-why-donors-give/.

Nonprofit Source. (2022). The Ultimate List Of Charitable Giving Statistics For 2022. https://nonprofitssource.com/online-giving-statistics/.

Orlando, A. (2021). 4 Nonprofit Fundraising Tips You'll Need in 2022. Donor Perfect. https://www.donorperfect.com/nonprofit-technology-blog/fundraising-software/strategize-by-season-4-nonprofit-fundraising-tips-youll-need-in-2022/.

Ostrower, F. (2005). Stanford Social Innovation Review. The Reality Underneath the Buzz of Partnerships. https://ssir.org/articles/entry/the_reality_underneath_the_buzz_of_partnerships.

Perrin, A. & Atske, S. (2021). About three-in-ten U.S. adults say they are 'almost constantly' online. Pew Research. https://www.pewresearch.org/fact-tank/2021/03/26/about-three-in-ten-u-s-adults-say-they-are-almost-constantly-online/.

Philanthropy News Digest. (2018). Recurring Donors 440 Percent More Valuable Than 'One-Off' Donors. https://philanthropynewsdigest.org/news/recurring-donors-440-percent-more-valuable-than-one-off-donors.

Statista. (2022). Most popular social networks worldwide as of January 2022, ranked by number of monthly active users. https://www.statista.com/statistics/272014/global-social-networks-ranked-by-number-of-users/.

Steel, Emily. (2014). Ice Bucket Challenge Has Raised Millions for ALS Association. The New York Times. http://nytimes.com/2014/08/18/business/ice-bucket-challenge-has-raised-millions-for-als-association.html.

Suttie. J., & Marsh, J. (2010). 5 Ways Giving is Good for You. Greater Good Magazine. https://greatergood.berkeley.edu/article/item/5_ways_giving_is_good_for_you.

Wordstream. (2022). Google Ads Benchmarks For Your Industry.
https://www.wordstream.com/blog/ws/2016/02/29/google-adwords-
    industry-benchmarks.

Made in United States
North Haven, CT
16 January 2024

47539490R00112